STEAM AROUND WOLVERHAMPTON

MIKE HITCHES

SUTTON PUBLISHING LIMITED

Sutton Publishing Limited
Phoenix Mill · Thrupp · Stroud
Gloucestershire · GL5 2BU

First published 1999

Title page photograph: LMS Stanier 2–6–2 tank No. 102 of Stafford shed, early 1930s.

British Library Cataloguing in Publication Data
A catalogue record for this book is available from the British Library.

ISBN 0-7509-2187-0

Typeset in 10.5/13.5 Photina.
Typesetting and origination by
Sutton Publishing Limited.
Printed in Great Britain by
Ebenezer Baylis, Worcester.

This book is dedicated to Hilary

ACKNOWLEDGEMENTS

I should like to record my grateful thanks to those organisations and individuals who have patiently assisted me in putting together this project, and without whose aid it would have been a very difficult work to attempt. My thanks go to Tracey Williams and the staff of the Archive at Wolverhampton Library, who managed to cope with my requests as I seemed to go through the place like a whirlwind – they must have wondered what this 'madman' was doing there. I should also like to thank the staff at Birmingham Reference Library for their valued assistance. Much material was also obtained from the pages of the *Wolverhampton Express and Star* and *Wolverhampton Chronicle* which provided valuable background information.

Individual assistance was freely given by Peter Owen, Roger Carpenter, F.W. 'Tim' Shuttleworth, David Ibbotson, Chris Hawkins, John Hooper and Arthur Truby, for which I am very grateful. Help was also provided by many anonymous people, often without realising it, and I thank them also.

Finally, my thanks go to my late wife Alwen and to Gary, who gave constant support in this and other projects.

CONTENTS

A broadside view of 'Castle' class 4–6–0 No. 7024 *Powis Castle* as she steams out of the shed yard at Stafford Road, late 1950s.

INTRODUCTION

An ancient hill town, Wolverhampton derived its name from Lady Wulfruna, who was sister to King Edgar of Mercia. She was granted land in Heantun (High Town) in 985 AD. This area became known, shortly afterwards, as Wulfruna's Heantun, which was later corrupted to Wolverhampton.

In the fourteenth and fifteenth centuries, the town became an important centre for the wool trade, which by the late eighteenth century was in terminal decline. However, the discovery of iron and coal in Staffordshire and North Worcestershire at about the same time was to bring a change of fortune to Wolverhampton. As these reserves of coal and iron were exploited in the area, which eventually became known as the Black Country because of its smoke-filled air and sooty deposits from the foundry and factory chimneys, Wolverhampton turned to production of iron-based goods.

In the same period, the first great transport revolution took place – canal construction, which allowed bulk transit of goods along specially constructed waterways. This led to sharp reductions in the price of coal and iron, and brought about rapid industrialisation in this part of the West Midlands. As canals were built to tap the great mineral wealth of the Black Country, Wolverhampton became an important transport centre because of its proximity to the Birmingham and Liverpool Junction Canal. The town itself was served by the Birmingham Canal Co. (after 1794 its name was changed to Birmingham Canal Navigations), which linked rapidly expanding Birmingham and the Black Country with Wolverhampton. The Staffordshire and Worcestershire Canal, opened in 1771, already linked Wolverhampton with the River Severn. Indeed, the Staffordshire and Worcestershire Canal company opened its head offices at Wolverhampton in 1772. The Birmingham Canal had been proposed in January 1767 and was opened between Wednesbury and Birmingham on 6 November 1769. The whole route through to Wolverhampton was completed on 14 September 1772 and opened to traffic seven days later. The canal's owners were often accused of breach of their own by-laws, illegal entry on to other people's property, monopoly over wharves and weighbridges and, most commonly, of levying high tolls for use of the canal and its facilities. From the Birmingham Canal other canals also came into existence to tap coal from the Black Country. These included the Stourbridge and Dudley Canals and the Wyrley and Essington Canal, all of which made Wolverhampton a major canal centre. The canal revolution was to be short-lived because the new railways, which crept up on the feuding canal owners almost unnoticed, eventually took most of the transport business away from them because they achieved faster delivery times and had the capacity to move larger quantities. However, the new railway routes in the Black Country, and Wolverhampton, tended to follow the course of the canals as their systems were developed. Despite severe damage to canal transport, transshipment between the canals and the railways continued to take place at Wolverhampton for over a century, and often formed the basis of disputes between competing railway companies in the early years.

As early as 1822, a survey was made by one William James for a railway from Wolverhampton to Birmingham, but the town did not appear on the railway map until the Grand Junction Railway's line between Earlestown, where it joined the Liverpool and Manchester Railway, and Birmingham, via Bescot, opened in 1837. The secretary of the GJR was the notorious Captain Mark Huish, who was to have a great influence on the structure of Wolverhampton's railway system. He made great attempts to thwart the development of competition with the London & North Western Railway, for whom he was to become General Manager. It could even be argued that Wolverhampton's railway system evolved in a complex way because of him. The GJR route passed through Wolverhampton, but the company viewed the town, perhaps surprisingly, as relatively unimportant at the time, and it was served by a small station at an inconvenient location; this station was called Wednesfield Heath from 1852.

From this insignificant beginning, Wolverhampton was to become one of the more important railway towns in Britain. It was also destined to become the subject of much political manoeuvring and corporate 'dirty tricks' as several railway companies vied with one another to become the most important to serve the town, and gain profit from the vast industrial wealth that was being generated in the nearby Black Country. This competition resulted in the creation of two important railway stations to serve Wolverhampton, several goods yards to deal with the huge quantities of freight traffic emanating from Black Country industries, an important locomotive construction and maintenance works and three large loco sheds.

Although never envisaged as such by the GJR, Wolverhampton became an important railway junction as rival companies built their routes into the town. By 1854, there were junctions at Stafford Road, where the Shrewsbury and Birmingham Railway met the GWR; Bushbury, where the Oxford, Worcester and Wolverhampton Railway met the GJR line between Stafford and Birmingham; Cannock Road, where the WJR (GW) left the OW&W to link up with the SB at Stafford Road (Priestfield to Bushbury was OW&W); and at Priestfield, where the GWR's Birmingham, Wolverhampton and Dudley Railway joined the OW&W from Dudley in order to enter Wolverhampton itself by running over OW&W metals.

There were bitter struggles at Wolverhampton between companies competing for routes from London, and the West Midlands, to Merseyside. The ambitions of the Shrewsbury & Birmingham Railway were curtailed at Wolverhampton, and two routes to Birmingham, which were to create a direct link to London, were approved by Parliament. This generated fierce competition between two mighty companies who had never been on friendly terms: the LNWR, whose Stour Valley line linked Birmingham with a High Level station at Wolverhampton; and the Great Western Railway, who built the mixed-gauge Birmingham, Wolverhampton & Dudley Railway from Snow Hill station, Birmingham, to Priestfield with running powers over the OW&W to Low Level station, Wolverhampton. Construction of a mixed-gauge line, which allowed the GWR to creep ever northward from Paddington to Merseyside with its 7-ft gauge, did little to calm the fears of the LNWR that the broad gauge would eventually reach its goal. Another contributing factor at Wolverhampton was the development of the OW&WR, who, initially, were on good terms with the GWR and its broad-gauge interests. Only later did the OW&WR turn against them and try to forge an alliance with their bitter enemy, the LNWR, causing the GWR many problems. All of these conflicting interests took several years to resolve, and led to the establishment of High and Low Level stations, both very different in character and both providing direct express services to London, via Birmingham, ensuring that a competitive edge would remain between the LNWR/LMS and GWR.

Eventually these disputes settled down and the railway companies concerned themselves with simply attracting business on an equal footing. Wolverhampton was provided with a railway system that ran services to destinations as far away as Scotland (no through trains beyond Glasgow or Edinburgh) and the south-west of England, as well as trains that served direct the capitals of England and Wales (no Wolverhampton–Cardiff service), along with boat trains to Holyhead for Dublin. The system included a comprehensive network of local trains throughout the Black Country, and other parts of the West Midlands. Also, the companies provided a variety of contrasting trains and locomotives which gave the railway enthusiast plenty to see and enjoy. This diversity continued until the mid–1960s, when the railway system at Wolverhampton was fully modernised, largely at the expense of the old GWR. The great range of steam locomotives were replaced by rather bland electric traction, which left the town without stabling and maintenance facilities as these were no longer required. The GWR station at Low Level also closed, traffic being concentrated at a new High Level station. Further, the old freight yards virtually disappeared, victims of the decline in goods traffic as road transport became more popular, and of Dr Beeching's report. All of these developments brought about great change in a system that had been in operation for well over a century.

In relating the story of the railways at Wolverhampton, I intend to detail some of the interesting facts for the railway enthusiast, as well as recording the turbulent and fascinating history of such an important, and often neglected, railway centre, one which truly was a railway crossroads.

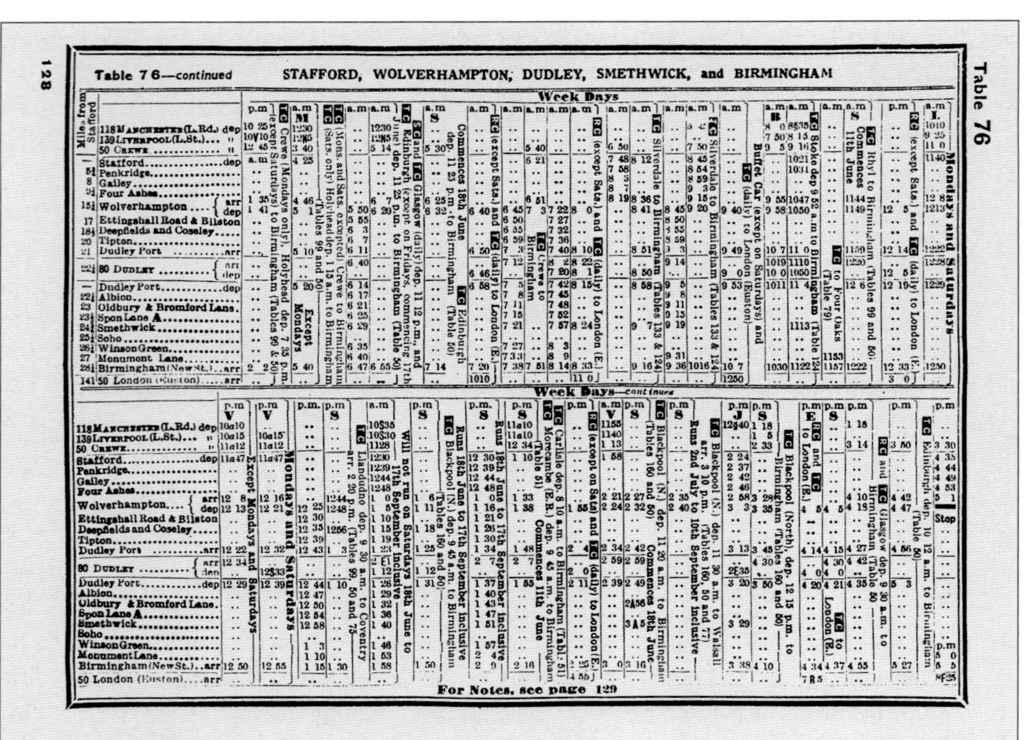

Table 76—continued STAFFORD, WOLVERHAMPTON, DUDLEY, SMETHWICK, and BIRMINGHAM

Week Days

Stations: 118 Manchester (L.Rd.) dep; 139 Liverpool (L.St.) dep; 50 Crewe dep; Stafford dep; Penkridge; Gailey; Four Ashes; Wolverhampton arr/dep; Ettingshall Road & Bilston; Deepfields and Coseley; Tipton; Dudley Port arr; 80 Dudley arr/dep; Dudley Port dep; Albion; Oldbury & Bromford Lane; Spon Lane A; Smethwick; Soho; Winson Green; Monument Lane; Birmingham (New St.) arr; 50 London (Euston) arr

Week Days—continued

For Notes, see page 129

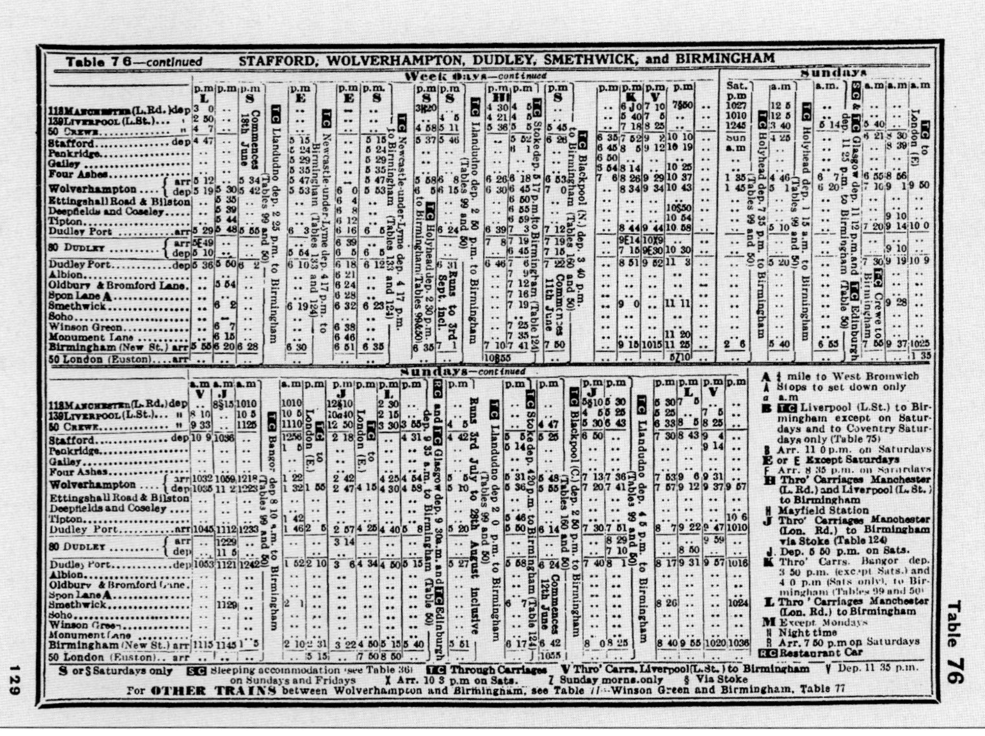

Table 76—continued STAFFORD, WOLVERHAMPTON, DUDLEY, SMETHWICK, and BIRMINGHAM

Week Days—continued | Sundays

Sundays—continued

A ¾ mile to West Bromwich
Ȧ Stops to set down only
a a.m
B TC Liverpool (L.St.) to Birmingham except on Saturdays and to Coventry Saturdays only (Table 75)
Arr. 11 0 p.m. on Saturdays
E or E Except Saturdays
F Arr. 8 35 p.m. on Saturdays
H Thro' Carriages Manchester (L. Rd.) and Liverpool (L. St.) to Birmingham
Mayfield Station
J Thro' Carriages Manchester (Lon. Rd.) to Birmingham via Stoke (Table 124)
J. Dep. 5 50 p.m. on Sats.
K Thro' Carrs. Bangor dep. 3 50 p.m. (except Sats.) and 4 0 p.m (Sats only), to Birmingham (Tables 99 and 50)
L Thro' Carriages Manchester (Lon. Rd.) to Birmingham
M Except Mondays
Night time
Arr. 7 50 p.m on Saturdays
RC Restaurant Car

S or S Saturdays only — SC Sleeping accommodation (see Table 36) on Sundays and Fridays — TC Through Carriages — V Thro' Carrs. Liverpool (L.St.) to Birmingham — V Dep. 11 35 p.m. — X Arr. 10 3 p.m on Sats. — Z Sunday morns. only — § Via Stoke

For OTHER TRAINS between Wolverhampton and Birmingham, see Table 77—Winson Green and Birmingham, Table 77

A 1946/47 winter timetable for local trains operating between Stafford and Birmingham, via Wolverhampton (High Level).

CHAPTER ONE

HIGH LEVEL AND THE LNWR

The shape of the railways at Wolverhampton were decided by several Acts of Parliament, which received Royal Assent on 3 August 1846. These included authorisation for the construction of the GWR-sponsored Birmingham, Wolverhampton & Dudley Railway, which became part of the GWR in 1848, the Oxford, Worcester & Wolverhampton Railway, and the Birmingham, Wolverhampton & Stour Valley Railway, as well as the Shrewsbury & Birmingham Railway. Construction of the latter two lines led to the establishment of a railway station at Queen Street, Wolverhampton, later to be known as High Level. Arguments over running powers for the S&B, the Stour Valley line and use of the Birmingham Canal for goods transport led to some of the fiercest disputes ever seen at Wolverhampton. This situation generated a great deal of revenue for the legal profession as these arguments went to litigation, and also resulted in law and order problems as disputes between the two companies involved led to physical violence.

The Birmingham, Wolverhampton & Stour Valley Railway, as authorised in 1846, formed only a small part of the original scheme devised by its S&B promoters. The S&B projected a line from Smethwick through the Stour Valley to Stourbridge and Stourport to connect with the River Severn. The whole route was never authorised so the 'Stour Valley' tag was always superfluous because the line never ran as far as the valley of the River Stour. What was authorised was a line from Birmingham (New Street) to a junction with the GJR at Bushbury. Also planned was a branch from Dudley Port to Dudley, which was already an established industrial centre in the Black Country. The concept of this line joining the London & Birmingham Railway and the GJR meant that it was in control of the LNWR from formation. Capital for construction came from four sources: the LNWR, S&B, the Birmingham Canal Co., whose own route ran parallel to the new line, and local interests. This arrangement frustrated the ambitions of the Euston-based LNWR, which would have preferred sole control so that it could improve its own network without interference and also be able to use the line as a political weapon to delay GWR interests in operating a through route to the Mersey. The S&B, having put up 25 per cent of the capital, held a quarter share in the new line and this resulted in some unpleasant arguments when the Stour Valley line was completed. The LNWR, however, managed to gain total control of the line by first negotiating a close financial and working agreement with the canal company and then by leasing the SVR in 1847; the S&B only had running powers over the new line.

Needing to check GWR-inspired plans to reach Wolverhampton, the LNWR decided that it would do without the SVR. However, it could not afford to delay construction because it was a duplicate, along with the GJR route, between Birmingham and Wolverhampton. The SVR to High Level was completed in 1851.

While the SVR was under construction, the S&B completed its own route and it was opened on 12 November 1849 to a temporary station in the town. Only a year later the first of many disputes with the LNWR arose over the use of the Birmingham Canal. The last ½ mile of the approach to High Level station was jointly owned with the LNWR and a line, built by the S&B into Victoria Basin, was the only place where transshipment of goods could take place. The LNWR did not want the S&B to use the basin and stirred up trouble to prevent them doing so. Further problems developed when the S&B wanted to use the SVR for access to Birmingham. As the LNWR did not want the line opened, it went to great lengths, both practically and legally, to prevent the S&B from using it. Such were the problems that eventually the S&B turned to the GWR to gain access to Birmingham and were warmly welcomed.

Alienation of the S&B gave the LNWR total control at High Level and a brand new station was opened there on 24 June 1852 and called Wolverhampton General. It was renamed Queen Street in September 1853 in recognition of the town's main road.

The frontage of Queen Street station (High Level), 1907. A station at High Level was first mentioned in *The Builder* on 13 September 1845 when it was announced that the railway companies passing through Wolverhampton were to unite in the construction of an important railway station as near to the town centre as possible, the bottom of Queen Street being the location for the joint terminus. The S&B had purchased the site on 29 September 1847 and the company's architect, Edward Banks, designed the new station, tenders for its construction being first published in March 1849. The entrance to the station was through a gated arch (not seen here) situated at the end of a 220-yd drive, which faced Wolverhampton's main thoroughfare, Queen Street. The station building had four archways: the centre pair for carriages, while the outer two were for pedestrians. Above these arches were the S&B offices and boardroom, while a row of shops was situated on either side of the entrance. This was the first part of the station to be opened, on 1 October 1849. Disputes between the S&B (which would eventually result in the S&B ceasing to use a station in which they were so involved) and the LNWR delayed further construction, and the station did not open properly until 24 June 1852. Even then tenders were still being invited for building of the station's refreshment rooms. The completed station was built of white brick, and a five-bay centrepiece with Corinthian pilasters surmounted by a dentilled pediment, which contained the town's coat of arms, was the main feature. The roof was constructed of iron and glass. By the time this photograph was taken, the disputes had been resolved and all three of the companies operating out of Wolverhampton are listed on the nameboard. Access to the GWR Low Level station was via a subway, the entrance of which was to the left of the main entrance. Note the variety of horse-drawn carriages, including several hansom cabs, in the main driveway.

The packed interior of High Level station and LNWR coaches, 1908. The station always suffered from insufficient accommodation and the LNWR proposed plans to extend the station. Unfortunately, these plans encroached on the public road to Low Level station and the GWR opposed the scheme. The town council also devised improvement schemes, which involved diversion of the approach road away from the arched entrance to a junction with the 1883-built Lichfield Street. As a result of these opposing plans and objections, work on station improvements did not begin until 1884. The reconstructed station remained in use until rebuilding was announced in the early 1960s.

An LNWR train has just arrived at High Level station to pick up passengers on the crowded platform, 1908.

The subway which linked the LNWR High Level station with the GWR Low Level station, the entrance to which can be seen on the extreme left of the picture on p. 10. In its early days, this subway was known as 'The Brothel' because of what took place there at night.

The LNWR viaduct which carried the Stour Valley line between High Level station and Bushbury, where it met the Grand Junction Railway line to Stafford and Crewe. The gas works is in front of the viaduct, with full gasholders behind, and the lines to Low Level and Herbert Street goods depot of the GWR are in the foreground. The rows of terraced houses are in Stafford Road, close to the GWR loco works.

The seven-arch railway viaduct at Penkridge, which lies between Wolverhampton (High Level) and Stafford on the GJR route, with an express passing through and a light engine resting on the viaduct. The loco appears to be an LNWR 0–6–0 goods engine and this picture was taken in LNWR days.

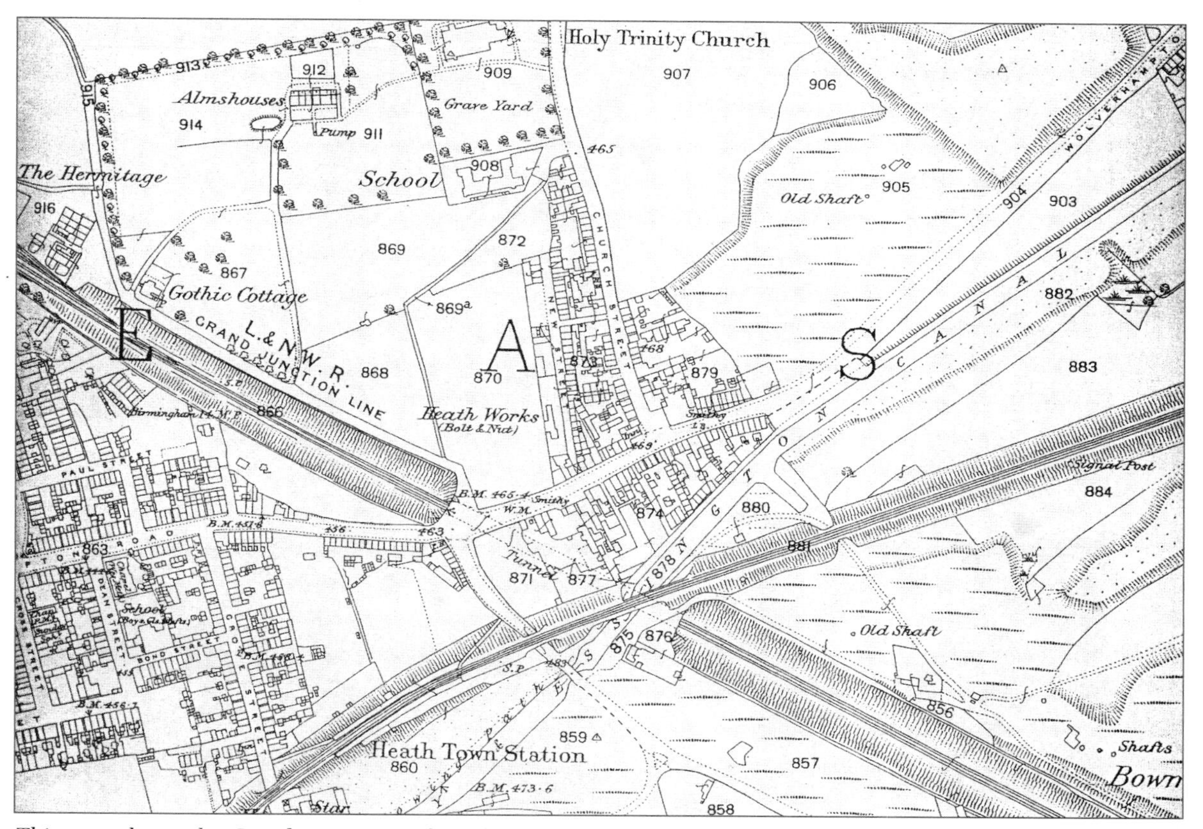

This map shows the Grand Junction Railway line as it passed through Heath Town at a point where the Midland Railway line from High Level to Walsall crossed above. The first railway to reach Wolverhampton was the Grand Junction, whose line was opened in 1837 and which became part of the LNWR in 1846. It was this line that the Euston company used as a weapon in its fight with the GWR and S&B when it refused to open the completed Stour Valley Railway. The GJR route, however, never passed through the centre of Wolverhampton and while the LNWR was in dispute with the S&B, passengers had to change trains at Bushbury, north of the town, and take another train into Wolverhampton itself, which was rather inconvenient.

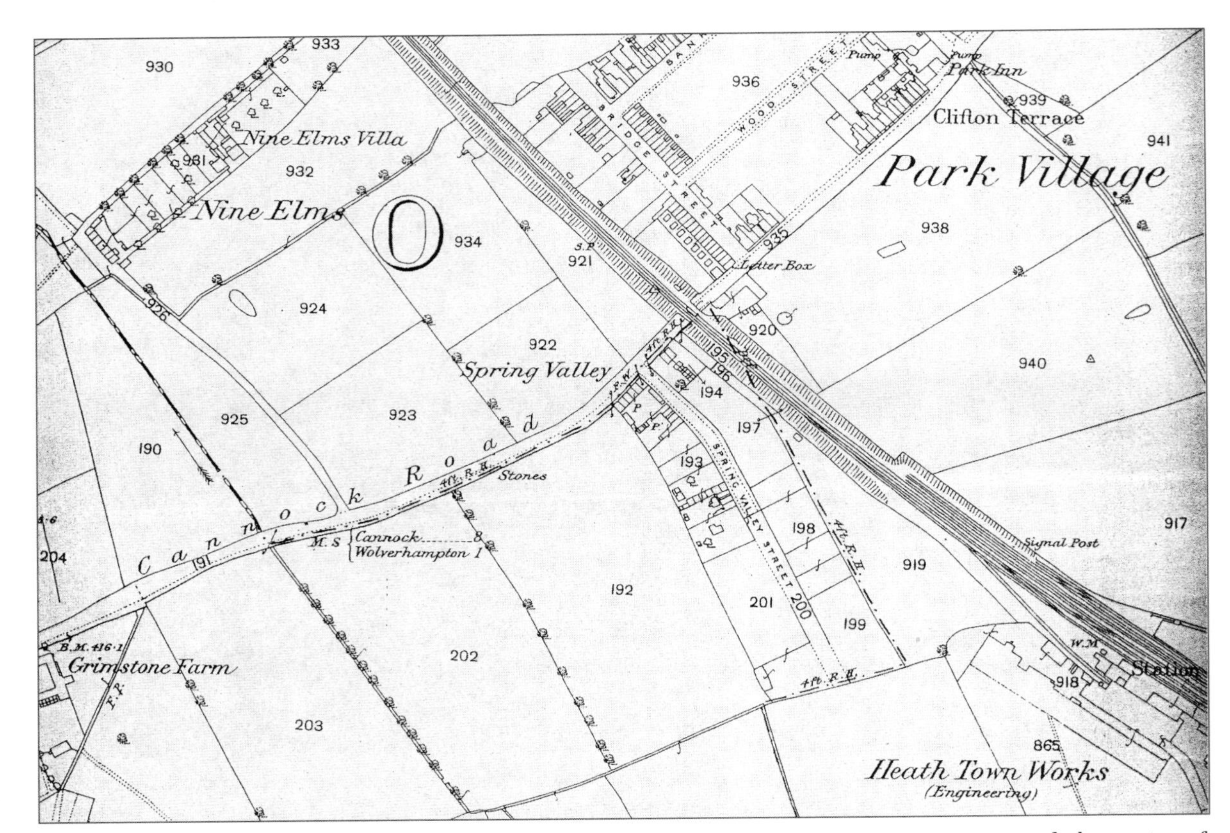

Part of the GJR line between Heath Town and Bushbury. It is clear that the GJR route missed the centre of Wolverhampton by some distance and the LNWR needed to have control of the Stour Valley line in order to shorten its route from Birmingham (New Street) and come closer to the town centre at High Level. This was particularly so as Mark Huish was becoming aware that the GWR would complete its line from Birmingham whatever measures he took to try to prevent it.

The exterior of Four Ashes station, on the GJR main line, in LNWR days. A local stopping train, headed by a 2–4–2 tank loco, is about to depart for Wolverhampton. Carriages wait for passengers who will alight from this particular train.

Four Ashes station on the GJR with a local train headed by ex-LMS Stanier 2–6–4 tank locomotive No. 42605 in BR days. Four Ashes station closed when the GJR was electrified.

Watford 0–6–2 tank loco LMS No. 7740 outside Bescot shed, 1935. This shed was an important GJR line loco shed as Bescot was a significant freight centre.

The final LNWR express design 4–6–0 locomotive as LMS No. 5948 *Baltic* of the 'Claughton' class outside Bescot shed. These locos were a familiar sight on LNWR expresses after the First World War and visited Wolverhampton's High Level station frequently.

Pictured on the GJR at Great Barr is the mainstay of heavy freight work, LNWR 'Super D' 0–8–0 No. 1012 with a long coal train. These engines were important for freight duties at Wolverhampton owing to the amount of heavy freight carried from the industrial Black Country. Both the LNWR and GWR benefited greatly from freight emanating from the area and both companies, along with the Midland Railway, had large goods yards in the town. Among other places, the LNWR had goods facilities close to High Level station and at Bushbury, while the GWR had a large freight yard at Oxley and goods facilities at Herbert Street and Victoria Basin. The Midland had two goods yards close to the Birmingham Canal, just south of High Level station and at Wednesfield Road.

The entrance to Albrighton station of the S&B, the first stop after Wolverhampton. Although the S&B was to fall into GWR hands, the company was instrumental in the establishment of High Level station and it was its arguments with the LNWR that were crucial to its uniting with the Paddington company. The S&B was opened on 12 November 1849 to a temporary station at Wolverhampton. Only a year later, and the little company was embroiled in its first conflict with the mighty LNWR when it tried to transship goods from its railway to the Birmingham Canal. The disagreement arose because the LNWR had joint ownership with the S&B of the last ½ mile of the approach to High Level station. This was the only section that ran beside the canal and the only place where transshipment was possible. The S&B had built lines into Victoria Basin, close to High Level station, for just this purpose. Problems, both legal and practical, started from the moment that the S&B attempted to lay a path of planks down the railway embankment so that goods could be transferred from the railway to the canal. The LNWR showed contempt for the legal position since access for the S&B was contained in the Act of Incorporation and safeguarded when the LNWR leased the Stour Valley line. The first clash occurred on 7 July 1850 when 300 navvies employed by Hoof, Hill and Moore, contractors for the SVR, met those of the S&B. A full-scale riot ensued and police, with soldiers, marched to the scene and the mayor read the 'Riot Act'. Later the same day several wagons were overturned further along the line and, after some stone throwing, police charged to disperse the rivals. Only a Chancery injunction curtailed the violence and the S&B were allowed to transfer goods at Victoria Basin. Following these events, the S&B sought a new route into Birmingham and developed closer ties with the GWR, whose own line from Birmingham to Wolverhampton was then under construction. The Shrewsbury & Chester Railway also experienced difficulties with Captain Mark Huish and the LNWR at Chester and wished to establish closer links with the GWR. Huish made several attempts to take over both of the Shrewsbury companies after negotiations with the GWR began through some dubious, and often illegal, moves but he failed. S&B shareholders agreed to a merger with the S&B and GWR, giving the Paddington company access to Chester and the Mersey, something that Huish had hoped to avoid. In the event, Huish made little attempt to prevent the S&B becoming part of the GWR, but was fiercely opposed to the S&C going the same way. Huish caused trouble at Chester and tried to prevent transshipment of goods from the Wirral line to Birkenhead, where access would be gained to the Mersey and the S&C. He even had the S&C ticket collector forcibly removed from Chester station. Huish went as far as attempting to set up an illegal Board of Directors of the S&C, but it was all to no avail and the two Shrewsbury companies merged with the GWR in 1852.

Oakengates station on the S&B. A tunnel collapse here led to delays in completing the line, but it was still opened while the SVR remained under construction. It was the LNWR policy of keeping the SVR closed that brought about another dispute with the S&B, which had a 25 per cent stake in the route to Birmingham. The S&B named 1 December 1852 as the date when it would start operating trains over the SVR to Birmingham (New Street). The LNWR stated that as the S&B had merged with the GWR it no longer had access to the SVR. The S&B went to litigation and won but the LNWR postponed opening, claiming that a hostile attempt to use the line would endanger public safety because of the possibility of collisions between S&B trains and their own. There was one problem that the S&B had not considered: the line approaching New Street was in the sole control of the LNWR which resulted in deadlock.

The station footbridge at Oakengates in WR days. Frustrated by the deadlock, the S&B resorted to force to gain access to the SVR and sent a train from High Level station. A short distance away, the train came buffer to buffer with LNWR loco *Swift*, which had been dispatched by the Euston company to block the progress of the S&B train. Hundreds of Wulfrunians gathered to watch the potentially explosive situation in the hope that there would be more fun and that police, along with troops, would be dispatched. On this occasion, however, the situation remained peaceful and only writs were exchanged. The outcome of this was that the LNWR agreed to review its position and the S&B consented not to try to force its way along the SVR. The S&B had plenty of local sympathy as Black Country businessmen wanted the SVR opened because its continued closure was causing hardship among the local population. In the end, the LNWR opened the SVR to goods traffic in February 1852 and to passengers five months later. The S&B was to pay a heavy price for access to New Street – the LNWR imposed a high rent for access. However, from 4 February 1854 S&B services began operating to New Street, although just three trains a day was a poor level of service.

Wellington station, operated, rather surprisingly, jointly by the GWR (having absorbed the S&B) and their rival the LNWR, who had a branch from Stafford. Locomotives of both companies are seen here: a GWR 2–6–2 Prairie tank and an LMS 2–6–4 tank. In complete disregard of an 1847 agreement, by which the LNWR took control of the Shropshire Union Railways and Canal Company (the line being that from Stafford to Wellington), the Euston company started a fare war with the S&B. The LNWR line was 46 miles long while the S&B route was only 29½ miles. The loss of a few thousand pounds was nothing to Huish if he could destroy the little Shrewsbury company and his pretext was that he had no right to make the 1847 agreement. The S&B took the matter to court and won but later lost on appeal, which delayed matters until 1851. At that time, passengers were carried between Wolverhampton and Shrewsbury at the low fare of 1*s* first class and 6*d* third class. As a comparison, fares between Wellington and Shrewsbury, over the joint line, were 6*d* first class and 1*d* third class for the 10½ miles.

Wellington station. As previously mentioned, the line from Wellington to Shrewsbury was jointly owned, the LNWR having control of the Shropshire Union which had originally owned the line. Despite everything that Captain Mark Huish could do, the GWR gained its route to the Mersey and, it could be argued, Huish brought the situation on himself by alienating the S&B and the S&C, who would have prevented the Paddington company going any further north than Wolverhampton.

Wellington station in BR days when it was part of the Western Region.

The entrance to Wellington Joint station, 1950s.

Coseley (Deepfields) station on the Stour Valley line from High Level to New Street. It was this route that the LNWR used as a weapon to keep the GWR out of Wolverhampton. Despite LNWR animosity to the broad-gauge GWR in its bid to reach Birmingham, the GWR began negotiations with the LNWR to try to establish running powers over the SVR and share New Street and High Level stations. The LNWR would have none of it, forcing the GWR to find its own way to Wolverhampton. To prevent the possibility of the GWR obtaining running powers through Parliament, the LNWR would not open its new line, relying on the GJR route for its traffic into Wolverhampton.

The SVR station at Great Bridge, Tipton, mid-1960s.

Wednesbury station on the SVR. The station appears to be in a dilapidated state, probably as a result of initial electrification work.

Smethwick station on the SVR, late 1950s.

Spon Lane station on the SVR, just before electrification was begun in the early 1960s.

Wolverhampton High Level station frontage just after nationalisation, 4 September 1949. The nameboards above the entrance show the two 'post-grouping' companies who operated trains from the town. At the end of the First World War, there was a demand for the railways to be nationalised, but the government of the day was politically opposed to state ownership during peacetime, although the railways had been under state control during the war. As a compromise, wholesale amalgamations were envisaged and the Railways Act of 19 August 1921 made provision for reorganisation of the railway companies into four groups, the change to take effect from 1 January 1923. At Wolverhampton, the LNWR and Midland Railway became part of the new London Midland & Scottish Railway, its trains still operating out of High Level, while the GWR retained its name and full identity.

An ex-LNWR 0–6–0 coal engine, used for freight work, is seen here as LMS No. 8308. In the early years of the grouping, LNWR engines remained the mainstay of traffic at Wolverhampton. Only the numbers changed and any LNWR emblems and names were removed to be replaced by 'LMS' lettering on tender sides, or tank sides on tank locos, until LMS replacements resulted in the withdrawal of the LNWR types.

Ex-LNWR 'Precursor' class 4–4–0 LMS No. 6334 at the head of a local passenger train.

Another ex-LNWR 0–6–0 coal engine LMS No. 8597 operating a three-coach local train.

Coal engine LMS No. 8597 at the head of a long local passenger train.

Ex-LNWR 0–6–2 coal tank LMS No. 6878 on a local passenger train in the Wolverhampton area.

Ex-LNWR 4–6–2 tank as LMS No. 6987 at the head of a local passenger train. It is interesting to note that the Midland Railway influence was strong in the early grouping years and engines were lettered and numbered in the 'Midland' style.

Another ex-LNWR 4–6–2 tank on a passenger service at Hednesford.

Ex-LNWR 4–4–2 tank LMS No. 8795 on a passenger train. These locos would have been a familiar sight on LNWR trains at High Level before the grouping.

Fowler 2–6–2 tank No. 18 on a local train. As the LMS settled down to build its own locos, old LNWR types were replaced by new LMS engines. Initially they were designed by ex-Midland Railway Chief Mechanical Engineer, Henry Fowler.

Another LMS Fowler 2–6–2 tank No. 17, still displaying 'Midland'-style numbering and lettering, on a local passenger train.

Fowler 2–6–2 tank No. 15518 at the head of a local train, early 1930s.

Fowler 2–6–2 tank No. 9 at the head of a local train.

Locos of the old Midland Railway began to appear on ex-LNWR lines after the grouping, as in this view of ex-MR 2P 4–4–0 at the head of a passenger train.

An early Stanier design, a 2–6–0 tender engine No. 2973, at the head of a local passenger train. In the 1930s, a new Chief Mechanical Engineer, William Stanier, was appointed to look after LMS locomotive affairs and he introduced his own locomotive styles, many of which became famous.

A Stanier 2–6–4 tank loco in post-Second World War lettering and numbering style as No. 2451 just before the LMS ceased to exist and a nationalised railway became the new order. Stanier's designs maintained LMS motive power through the Second World War and into the nationalised era.

Still in LMS livery and painted in the company's crimson lake colours, horse-drawn van No. 4990 is outside Craddock's shoe factory, Snow Hill, 18 September 1952. Wolverhampton's railways thrived on the sheer quantity of goods traffic emanating from the town and nearby Black Country. As 'common-carriers', however, they were obliged to carry anything from heavy plant to small parcels, the latter requiring delivery from the goods yard to the customer, usually by lorry or, as in this case, by horse-drawn van.

CHAPTER TWO

LOW LEVEL AND THE GWR

While Wolverhampton had been reached first by the GJR, it was to become a GWR town, though never a Divisional Headquarters, except for locomotives and civil engineering. From 1855, the GWR's Northern Division stretched from Birmingham to Chester and was controlled from Shrewsbury. The headquarters moved to Chester in 1861 following creation of a new division for the Birmingham area which included Wolverhampton, the boundary being established just north of the town. Besides being the southern terminus of the S&B and the northern terminus of the BW&D, it was also the terminus of the OW&W.

The Oxford, Worcester & Wolverhampton Railway to Low Level was the first line to be constructed but it took nine years to build the 89¼-mile route from north of Oxford to the Wolverhampton terminus, which was situated some 30 ft below the High Level station. In the early years, following the company's incorporation, some work was carried out in the vicinity of Wolverhampton including the start of tunnel excavation at Dudley. By the end of 1846 work progressed south of Tipton but nothing was done further north because of plans, which were finally authorised on 14 August 1848, for a 2½-mile diversion of the northern section to Wolverhampton Low Level to be built jointly with the S&B and Birmingham, Wolverhampton & Dudley Railway. It was agreed that if the S&B was sold, leased or transferred to the LNWR, as seemed likely thanks to the efforts of Captain Mark Huish, its share was to be absorbed by the other partners. The Act that authorised these plans also switched the junction with the GJR from Wednesfield Heath to Bushbury.

The BW&D reached neither Wolverhampton nor Dudley. Its main line terminated at Priestfield, more than a mile from Low Level station, where it joined the OW&W to gain access to Wolverhampton. At the time the OW&W was regarded as a loyal member of the broad-gauge camp and was leased to the GWR. In 1851, when the construction of the BW&D was under way, the OW&W was in serious conflict with the GWR. The OW&W went as far as proposing to abandon its own line to Wolverhampton and reach the town by running over the Stour Valley line from a junction at Tipton. The Stour Valley line was owned by the LNWR, who were delighted to have a good chance to thwart the GWR's ambition to reach the town. The OW&W even built a narrow gauge line to connect with the LNWR's Stour Valley line.

Fearing that any arrangement with the LNWR would leave the BW&D isolated at Priestfield, the GWR applied to Parliament in 1852 for permission to build this portion of the OW&W itself. Parliament rejected this but forced the OW&W to build a mixed-gauge line from Priestfield to Wolverhampton and on to a point known as Cannock Road Junction, about ½ mile north of the station towards Bushbury. The OW&W was also threatened with heavy penalties if they did not complete their mixed-gauge line by September 1853. While the OW&W did not easily concede, the GWR obtained its running powers a year later. In the same parliamentary session that forced the OW&W to complete its line, the GWR gained authorisation to build a line which brought the S&B into Low Level station. The OW&W line opened to passengers on 1 July 1854 to a temporary station at Low Level.

The BW&D from Birmingham (Snow Hill) to Priestfield was opened on Tuesday 14 November 1854, along with the junction with the S&B at Wolverhampton, which gave the GWR a through route from Birmingham to Shrewsbury. The BW&D was of mixed gauge, while the S&B was standard gauge; thus the GWR broad gauge went no further than Wolverhampton.

Amalgamation with the S&B and S&C provided the GWR with its route to the Mersey, something that the LNWR had fought so hard to avoid because it would mean it would lose its monopoly of Liverpool sea port traffic.

Churchward 2–6–2 Prairie tank No. 4528 with inside steam pipes at the GWR Low Level station, 1924. The station was designed by engineers of the three companies that planned to use it: the station buildings were designed by John Fowler of the OW&W, the roof by I.K. Brunel of the GWR and the track and platform layout were devised by Henry Robertson of the S&B.

Night Express Goods Trains at Wolverhampton

These night express goods trains were generally hauled by 47XX class 2–8–0 goods locomotives, Oxley shed having an allocation for this work. These trains were given nicknames by GWR staff, which were officially adopted by the company from 1929 as a way of attracting traders and industry to use the services offered. A list of these trains from, to and through to Wolverhampton are given below.

From Wolverhampton

Time	Name	Destination
1.30 a.m.	'The Southern Docker'	Basingstoke
2.10 a.m.	'The Southerner'	Basingstoke
2.45 a.m.	'The Northern Docker'	Birkenhead
4.00 a.m.	'The Northern Exchange'	Crewe
8.15 p.m.	'The Racer'	Paddington
10.15 p.m.	'The Crosser'	Westbury
12.45 a.m.	'The Flying Skipper'	Birkenhead
7.10 a.m.	'The Cargo'	Basingstoke (from Victoria Basin)

To Wolverhampton

Time	Name	From
2.10 a.m.	'The Cherbourg'	Basingstoke
9.35 p.m.	'The BBC'	Basingstoke
9.20 p.m.	'The Western Docker'	Bristol
8.25 p.m.	'The Early Riser'	Manchester
11.05 p.m.	'The Hampton'	Paddington
4.20 a.m.	'The Moonraker'	Westbury
7.22 a.m.	'The Drayton'	West Drayton

Through Wolverhampton

Time	Name	Route
3.55 p.m.	'The Meat'	Birkenhead–Smithfield
8.20 p.m.	'The General'	Birkenhead–Paddington
10.50 p.m.	'The Birmingham Market'	Birkenhead–Bordesley Junction
11.35 p.m.	'The Cambrian Pioneer'	Birkenhead–Oswestry
9.10 p.m.	'The Shipper'	Bordesley Junction–Birkenhead
6.50 p.m.	'The Farmer's Boy'	Bristol–Birkenhead
7.45 p.m.	'The Mon'	Manchester–Bristol
9.10 p.m.	'Northern Flash'	Paddington–Birkenhead
11.40 p.m.	'The Grocer'	Southall–Crewe
7.35 p.m.	'The Lancashire Lad'	Westbury–Manchester

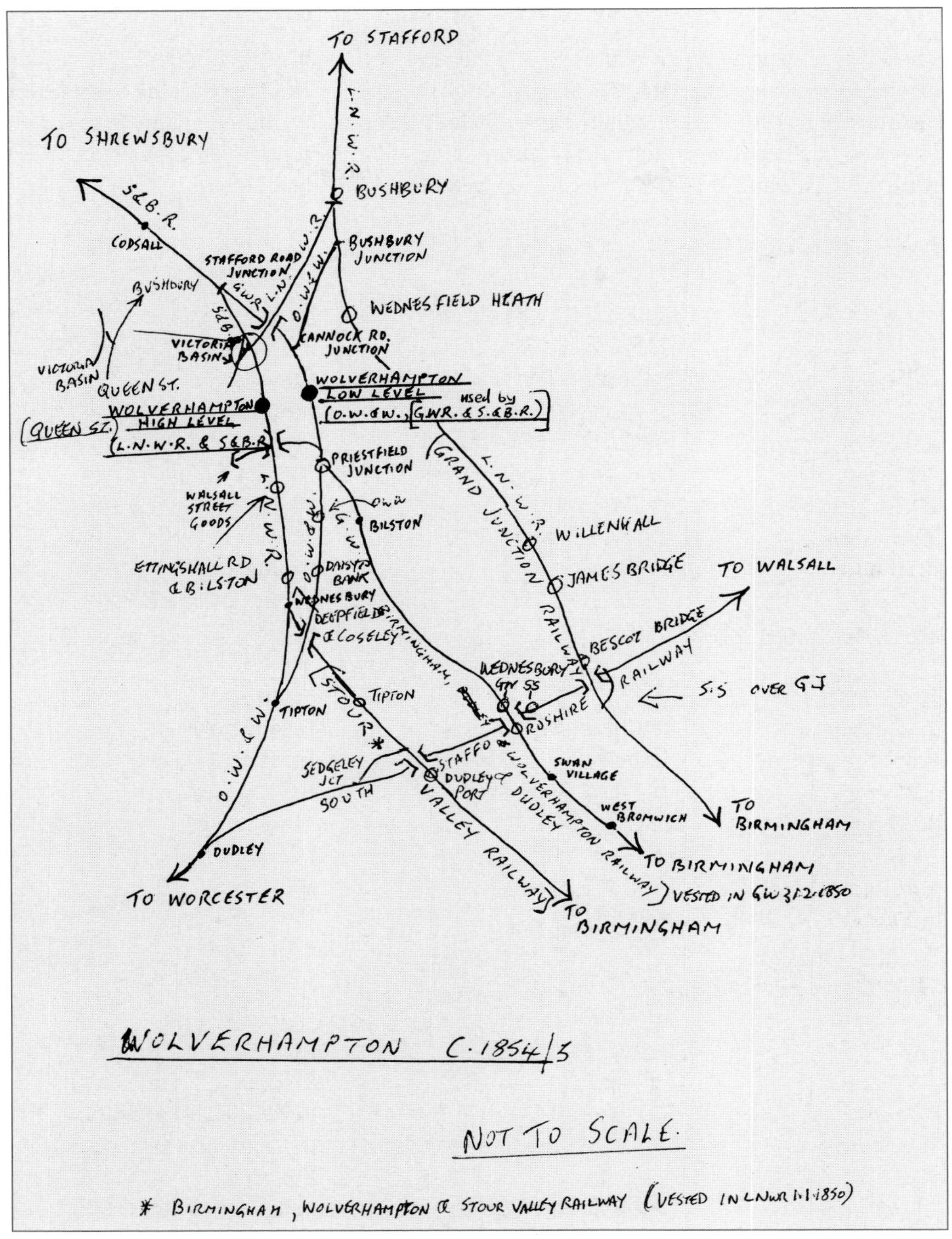

A plan of the railway system at Wolverhampton showing the lines that served the town, *c.* 1854. At that time, the S&B had access to both Low and High Level stations because of its running powers over the Stour Valley Railway, belonging to the LNWR, and the company's merger with the GWR, which allowed access to Low Level. The S&B ceased using High Level after trains were transferred to the Snow Hill route and through trains from Euston via Yarnton were discontinued on 1 October 1861, which gave the LNWR sole control at High Level. Low Level station was, at that time, shared by the OW&W and GWR as well as the S&B. The GWR gained sole control of Low Level station after they took over the West Midland Railway on 1 August 1863, the OW&W having become part of the WMR in 1860.

Dunstall Park station on the Wolverhampton Junction Railway, which brought the S&B into Low Level. The GWR opened Dunstall Park as an intermediate station on 1 December 1896 and the station was to have an important role because it dealt with a lot of railway traffic for the nearby racecourse.

Dunstall Park station, which lay very close to the GWR loco works at Stafford Road, 1967. The works can be seen nestling against the station platform.

Prince's End and Coseley station on the OW&W line between Wolverhampton and Dudley. The OW&W's was the first route constructed into Low Level station, and was another source of conflict in the area. The BW&D line from Birmingham (Snow Hill) joined the OW&W at Priestfield for access into Wolverhampton, but the Oxford company had become friendly with the LNWR and plans were made to bring the line from Oxford into High Level station. Only litigation on the part of the GWR, as lessees of the BW&D, forced the OW&W to complete its line into Low Level. The action taken by the GWR left the OW&W rather bitter, and the company maintained friendly relations with the LNWR until it became part of the West Midland Railway in 1860.

The OW&W station at Great Bridge (Tipton). In the nine years it took to complete the line from Oxford, the OW&W often ran into financial trouble and when the line opened it was a ramshackle affair. It became known as the 'Old Worse and Worse' because of the state of its locos and rolling stock, as well as the unreliability of its services. The OW&W was absorbed by the GWR on 1 August 1863, having become part of the West Midland Railway in 1860.

Dudley station, the first major station on the OW&W from Wolverhampton, in GWR days. The OW&W was the first railway company to build a line that included Dudley on its route. The line was given Royal Assent on 4 August 1845 despite strong opposition from the London & Birmingham Railway, whose monopoly in the Birmingham area would be undermined. Originally, the line was intended to be broad gauge, but financial problems and disputes with the GWR, who were acting as guarantors, meant that it was finally built in standard gauge after friendly relations with the LNWR developed. There was even agreement that the LNWR and Midland Railway would operate OW&W trains. It was not until 20 December 1852 that a 6-mile section of single line opened between Stourbridge and Dudley, starting from Brettell Lane. By 1853 one freight and five passenger trains were running on weekdays, with two passenger trains on Sundays, from Dudley to Handborough and back. At the end of 1853 the OW&W line from Dudley ran to a junction with the LNWR Stour Valley line at Tipton, disputes with the GWR allowing the LNWR to work trains between Dudley and its own station at Wolverhampton in 1855. Dudley station was also the destination of the South Staffordshire Railway, which arrived there in 1849 and was absorbed by the LNWR in 1867. Thus, Dudley station became jointly owned by the GWR and its old foe the LNWR.

A GWR rail car unloading passengers and taking on parcels at Dudley station. The GWR experimented with diesels on local and express services from the mid-1930s.

A GWR rail car waits at Dudley station, 1930s. The GWR and LMS began to experiment with alternative traction to steam in the 1930s, and even the Southern Railway was using electric traction at that time. Such trials ceased when the Second World War broke out and the railways were so short of cash when the war was over that the challenges of alternative traction could no longer be pursued. This prolonged the life of steam traction much longer than would otherwise have been the case.

A GWR 2–6–2 Prairie tank enters Dudley station with a passenger train from Wolverhampton (Low Level).

Station staff, including a young lad, pose on the original OW&W station at Stourbridge Junction, which closed in 1901. It was between here and Dudley that the first OW&W trains ran.

A local train, headed by what appears to be a 'Dean Goods' 0–6–0 locomotive, complete with polished brass dome (a feature of Dean engines), waits at Stourbridge Junction station, *c.* 1910. The original Stourbridge Junction station was replaced in 1901 by the one seen here, which has typical GWR architecture; the OW&W line was part of the Paddington empire at the time. Stourbridge has long been an important Black Country town and is famous for glass production. Such was its prosperity in the nineteenth century that it soon attracted the interest of the major railway companies who were keen to link the town with the larger commercial centre of Wolverhampton. The first company to show interest was the Birmingham, Wolverhampton & Stour Valley Railway, promoted by the S&B in the early 1840s, which would have put the town under LNWR control. However, the town came under the jurisdiction of the GWR after it took charge of the OW&W.

Double-framed Dean 4–4–0 No. 3444 heads an express made up of red GWR coaches through Stourbridge Junction on its way from Worcester to Wolverhampton (Low Level) soon after the First World War. The 1923 grouping was to have little effect on the Paddington company as it only absorbed small lines in South Wales and did not have its name changed.

Another view of the GWR station at Stourbridge Junction in BR days.

Stourbridge Junction, late 1950s. The typical GWR station canopies are clearly seen and in the background is a DMU train, which replaced steam on local services as part of the 1955 'Modernisation Plan'.

Stourbridge Town station. Stourbridge town centre lay about a mile away from Stourbridge Junction station and in 1865 the Stourbridge Railway obtained the right to construct a branch into the town but these powers lapsed before construction could begin. The GWR acquired a fresh Act in 1874, but five years passed before the branch was completed. Just beyond the station, goods facilities were provided at Stourbridge Basin. A shuttle service between the Town station and Stourbridge Junction was operated to enable passengers to make the connection with the main line for trains to Worcester and Wolverhampton (Low Level).

Bilston Central station on the BW&D line just south of Priestfield Junction. This line was authorised in the same year as the LNWR Stour Valley Railway but construction did not commence until 1851, as the GWR had entered into negotiations with the LNWR to try to gain access to Birmingham (New Street) and the Stour Valley line. Not surprisingly, these talks failed and the LNWR tried everything in its power to prevent the GWR reaching Wolverhampton. The LNWR even went as far as refusing to open its own Stour Valley route in case the Paddington company sought running powers over it. The BW&D was built as a mixed-gauge line because the S&B, which amalgamated with the GWR, was standard gauge and the LNWR had forced the GWR to lay mixed-gauge track from Leamington to Birmingham (Snow Hill). The BW&D was a continuation line from Birmingham (Snow Hill) to Wolverhampton (Low Level) where it met the S&B line to Shrewsbury and the north-west.

Another view of the BW&D station at Bilston Central in BR days.

Wednesbury station on the BW&D. The line between Birmingham (Snow Hill) and Priestfield was engineered by J.R. McLean, who was also engineer and lessee of the South Staffordshire Railway, whose line went to Dudley instead of the BW&D. After some delays, the line was ready for inspection in August 1854. Unfortunately, on 26 August, a bridge between Soho and Handsworth collapsed, delaying opening of the line until November. The GWR, who took control of the BW&D before the line was finished, now competed directly with the LNWR for traffic between London and the north-west of England.

A GWR 2–4–0 locomotive, No. 214, built locally at Wolverhampton's Stafford Road works, waits with a passenger train at Wednesbury, 1905.

An Edwardian view of West Bromwich station on the BW&D. Note the children waiting patiently on the platform.

The BW&D station of Smethwick and Handsworth, 1950s.

Smethwick West station, 1950s. This station was on the GWR line from Smethwick Junction to Stourbridge, Hagley, Kidderminster and Worcester (Shrub Hill). The line linked the BW&D with the CW&W at Stourbridge Junction.

Another station on the line to Stourbridge was at Rowley Regis and Blackheath, seen here on a very busy day before the First World War. The coaches seen here are a mixture of GWR chocolate and cream and red, introduced by Churchward as an economy measure.

TO SHREWSBURY
OXLEY
OXLEY NORTH JCN.
OXLEY BRANCH JCN.
OXLEY MIDDLE JCN.
TETTENHALL
WOLVERHAMPTON
COMPTON HALT
PENN HALT
N
WOMBOURN
PROPOSED LINE TO BRIDGNORTH (1913)
HIMLEY
TO WOLVERHAMPTON
TO WALSALL
GORNAL HALT
DUDLEY
PENSNETT HALT
BLOWERS GREEN
NETHERTON
BROMLEY HALT
BLOWERS GREEN JCN.
BROCKMOOR HALT
BRIERLEY HILL
"THE BUMBLE HOLE"
BRETTELL LANE
TO STOURBRIDGE JCN.
THE WOMBOURN BRANCH (OPENED BY THE GWR IN 1925) & ITS CONNECTIONS (NOT TO SCALE)

A map of the Wombourn Branch opened by the GWR in 1925. This was the only line actually built by the Paddington company in the Wolverhampton area. The branch left the S&B main line at Oxley and ran through to Brettell Lane, where it met the OW&W between Stourbridge Junction and Dudley. A line from Wombourn to Bridgnorth, now home of the famous preserved Severn Valley Railway, was proposed in 1913 but never actually built.

Tettenhall station on the GWR branch between Oxley and Brettell Lane, which was opened on 11 May 1925. The route was 12 miles long and was single with a passing loop at Wombourn. Steam rail motors were used over the route but passenger numbers never lived up to expectations and the branch only survived as a passenger route until 31 October 1932.

Tettenhall station, 19 September 1965. Although closed to passengers in 1932, the station buildings survived for many years.

Wombourn station on the Oxley–Brettell Lane branch, shortly after opening with the new branch. After closure to passengers, the line remained open for freight until complete closure in 1965. This small line proved useful as a bypass route, avoiding Wolverhampton and Birmingham, during the Second World War.

'Atlantic' 4–4–2 locomotive No. 104 *Alliance*, Wolverhampton (Low Level) station, 1924. *Alliance* was one of two French Compounds bought for the GWR by G.J. Churchward in 1905. These locomotives were similar to Paris–Orleans 3001 class and were modified to suit the GWR loading gauge. They were bought to compare Compound with simple expansion locomotives and these experiments were to produce the famous 'Star' and 'Saint' class 4–6–0s. By the time this picture was taken, the engine had been rebuilt and fitted with a standard GWR boiler. It was a familiar sight on Wolverhampton–Paddington trains of the day. The station roof, just visible in this view and which was 575 ft long overall and built of iron and glass weighing 400 tons, was suffering the effects of corrosion by 1923, and despite repairs being carried out it continued to deteriorate. The GWR was left with little choice but to remove it. On 2 October, contractors Wilson, Lovatt and Co. began work on dismantling the overall roof, the work being completed, with little interruption to traffic, by early May 1934. Standard GWR canopies were placed over the platforms as work progressed.

Low Level station after the overall roof had been removed, showing the canopies that replaced it. Other work carried out included replacing gas lighting with electricity in March 1930. High Level station continued to be gas lit until it was rebuilt in 1962. The GWR also carried out improvements to its goods yards at that time.

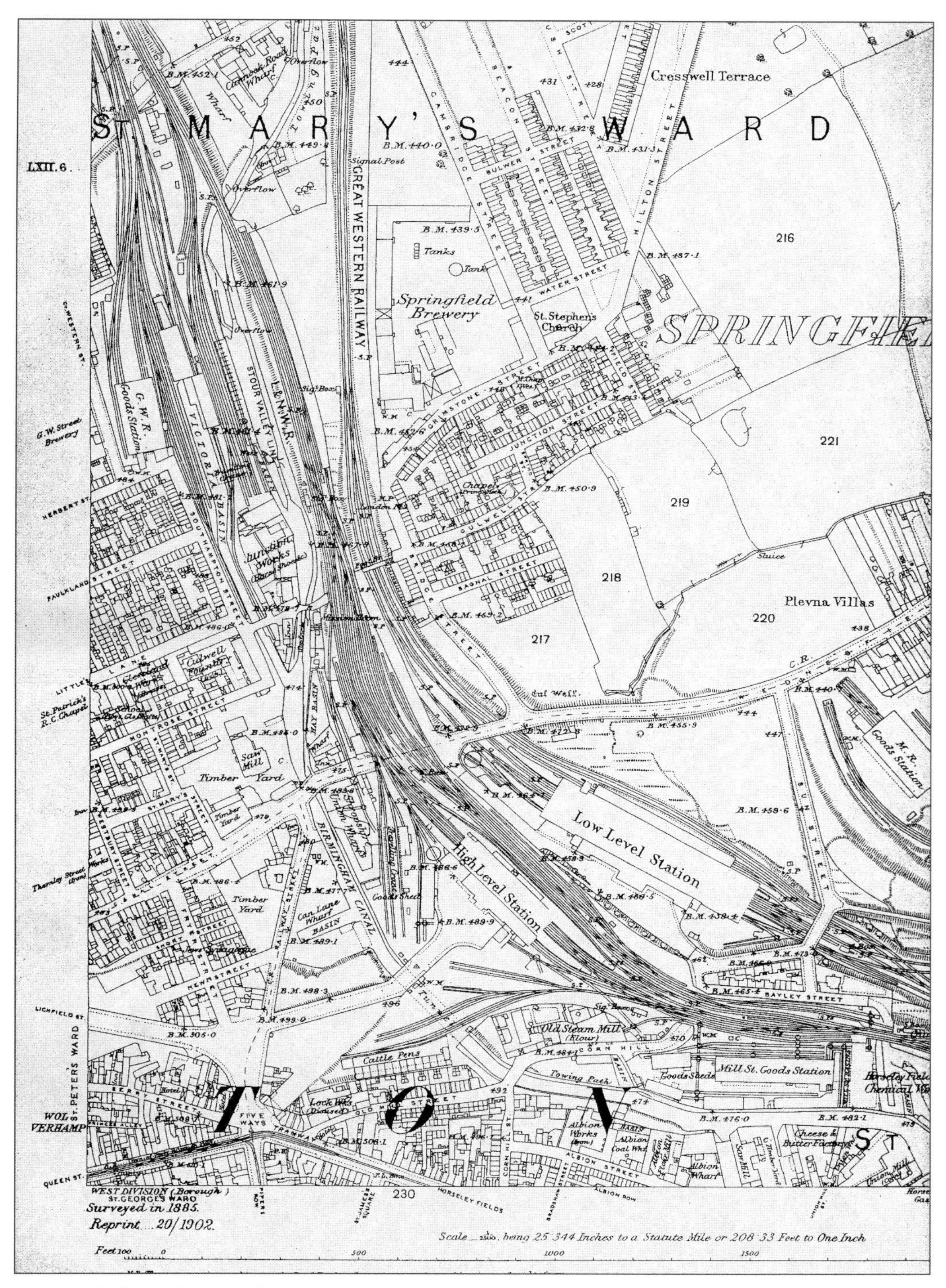

A map of the railway and stations at Wolverhampton showing the complex of main lines, freight yards and sidings that served the town. Seen here are the two stations at Wolverhampton, the LNWR goods sidings behind High Level station and the Stour Valley line as it progresses towards Bushbury. Also detailed are the GWR (S&B) line heading towards Shrewsbury, the Paddington company's goods yard at Herbert Street and the ex-S&B goods sidings at Victoria Basin, the site of their original dispute with the LNWR.

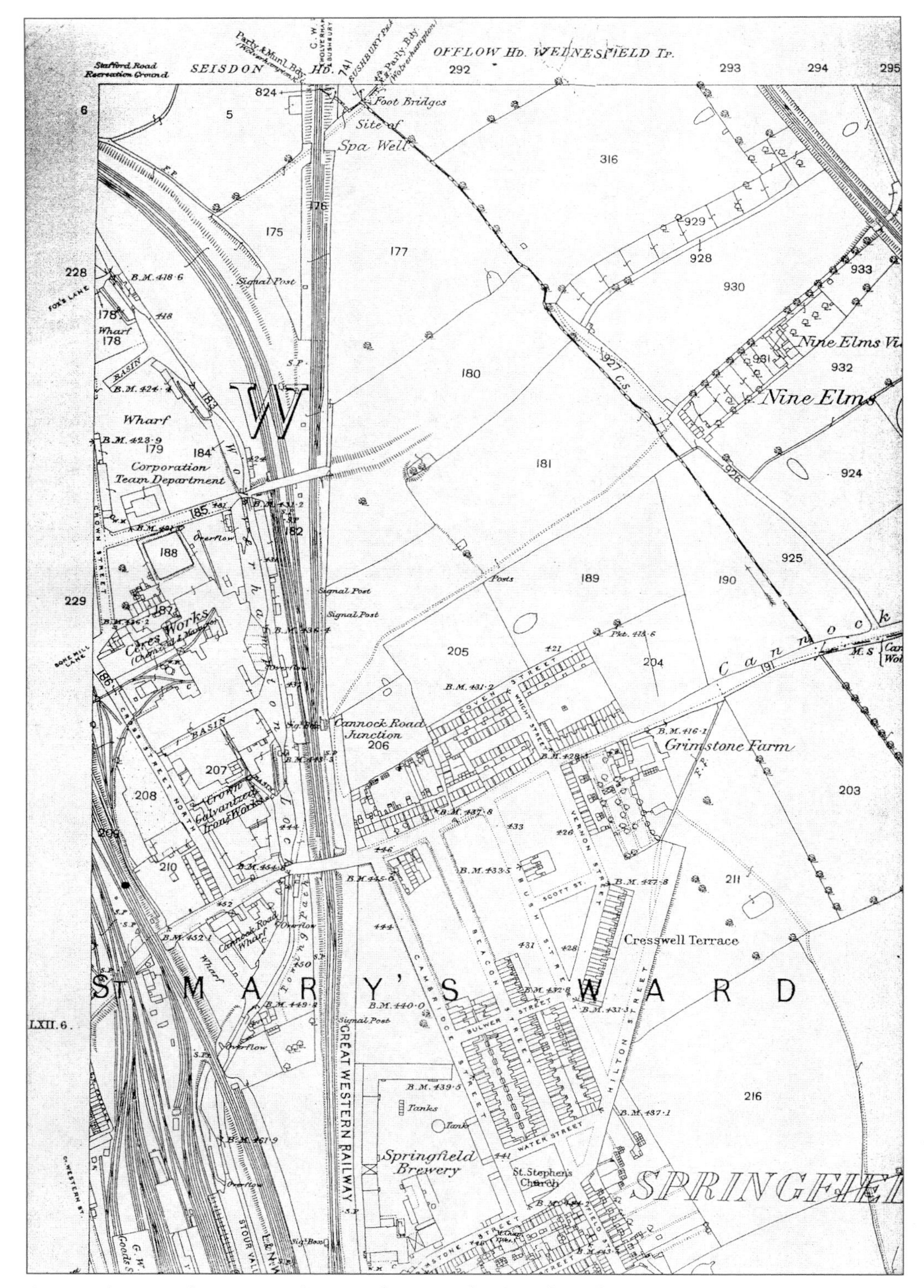

A map showing the GWR and LNWR lines north of High and Low Level stations. At Cannock Road Junction, the Shrewsbury line curves away to the left.

An experimental Diesel Multiple Unit three-car set, built as an AEC/Leyland joint venture in 1952, at Priestfield station, 18 August 1953. This is the point where the BW&D met the OW&W, whose line can be seen going off to the right, and where the GWR clashed with the Oxford company over access to Low Level station after the OW&W had become friendly with Captain Huish's LNWR.

A passenger's view of Oxley Middle Junction, on the S&B line to Shrewsbury, 1956. The Wombourn branch veers off to the left. The train is a Talyllyn Special to Mid Wales, headed by ex-LMS three-cylinder Compound 4–4–0 No. 41123.

CHAPTER THREE

THE MIDLAND RAILWAY

Once the arguments between the railway companies had been resolved, rail provision at Wolverhampton was dominated by two companies, the GWR and LNWR. However, the Midland Railway managed to gain a toe-hold in the town, but only through the consent of the LNWR, with whom the Midland were on very friendly terms. Unlike Birmingham, where the Midland ranked second behind the LNWR with the GWR third, the company only had a very minor role at Wolverhampton.

The GWR and LNWR having settled their differences, improvements were made to the railway systems in the area and gaps were filled in, such as the one between Wolverhampton, Willenhall and Walsall. Willenhall was, and still is, an important lock-manufacturing centre lying some 3 miles east of Wolverhampton, and Walsall was a major centre for leather goods, which meant that both towns were useful for freight and passenger traffic. Incorporation of the Wolverhampton & Walsall Railway, on 29 June 1865, was to provide the route to Willenhall and Walsall, but the 8-mile line took seven years to build, four additional Acts being required for time extensions or modifications. One of these Acts transferred the junction at Wolverhampton from the GWR Low-Level line to the Stour Valley route because the LNWR and Midland planned to work the Wolverhampton & Walsall Railway individually rather than jointly from its opening, which took place on 1 November 1872.

Three years after opening the W&W was purchased by the LNWR and sold to their close friends, the Midland, a year later. The Midland had already reached Walsall from the opposite direction, with a line from Castle Bromwich, as a result of absorbing the Wolverhampton, Walsall & Midland Junction Railway in 1874. It was, therefore, natural that the Midland should have control of the W&W and create a direct link between Wolverhampton and the Midland main line between Derby and Birmingham.

The LNWR opened its own Wolverhampton and Walsall route on 1 March 1881 after completion of two important curves. These were between the GJR line and the South Staffordshire Railway, which ran from Wichnor Junction to Dudley, via Pleck; and between the GJR at Portobello Junction and the Midland at Heath Town Junction. From 1 January 1909, Midland trains switched to the LNWR route between Walsall and Wolverhampton and some LNWR services began using the Midland route (there were Willenhall stations on both routes) to avoid reversal.

With the arrival of the Midland Railway the railway map at Wolverhampton was complete. The GWR was the largest and most important company, the LNWR was comfortably in second place, while the Midland played only a small but necessary part.

Ex-LNWR 'Super D' 0–8–0 No. 49328 works a freight train over the Midland Railway line from Walsall to High Level, 20 March 1955. The train will run through to the large ex-GWR sidings, opened in 1907, at Oxley. Visible on the right is the Midland goods yard at Wednesfield Road and High Level station can be seen in the middle distance.

The former Midland Railway's goods depot at Wednesfield Road with a pair of ex-LNWR 'Super D' 0–8–0s of Bescot shed on duty, 1950s.

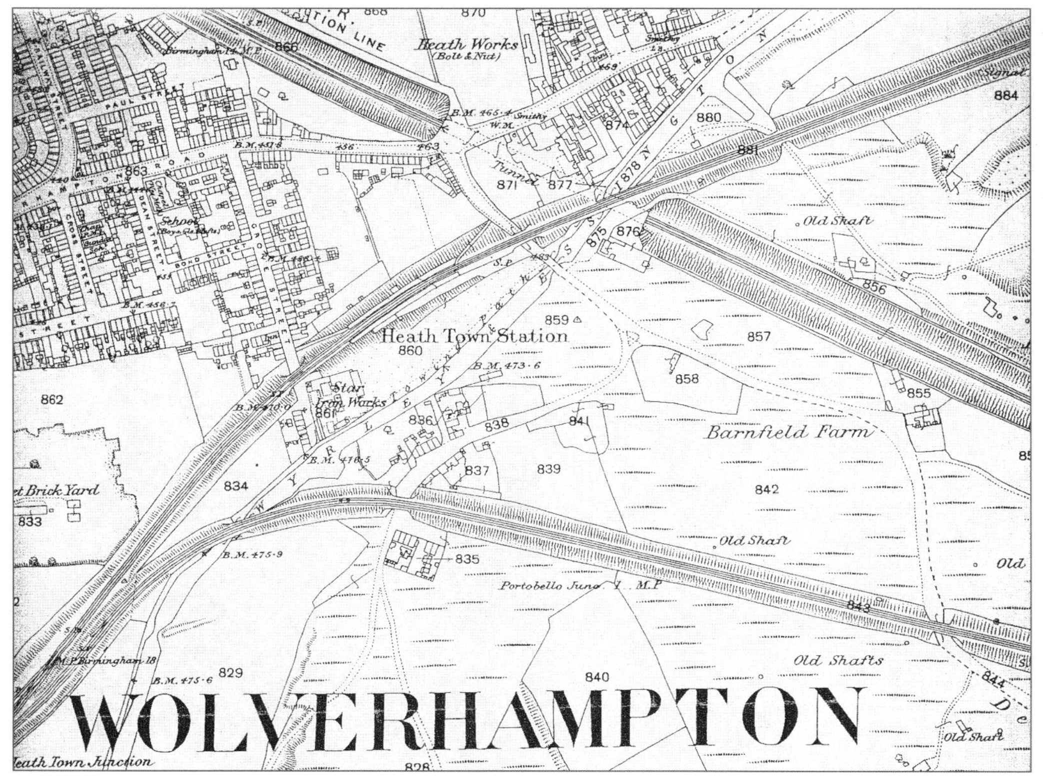

A map of the Midland Railway line from Wolverhampton to Walsall at Heath Town detailing the point where it crossed above the Grand Junction Railway line to Bushbury.

A map showing the Midland Railway goods depot at Wednesfield Road with its complex of sidings and the goods station. The Midland line from High Level to Walsall passes close by and the entrance to the goods yard can be seen at Freeman Street.

ʼidland Railway double-arm home signals at Heath 'own on the bridge which crossed the GJR main line, . 1957.

An excursion train on the Midland line from Wolverhampton (High Level) to Walsall, at Aldridge, run by th Stephenson Locomotive Society, shortly before closure in 1963.

A view of the same excursion train showing the locomotive, an ex-LMS 2–6–4 tank, sandwiched in the middle.

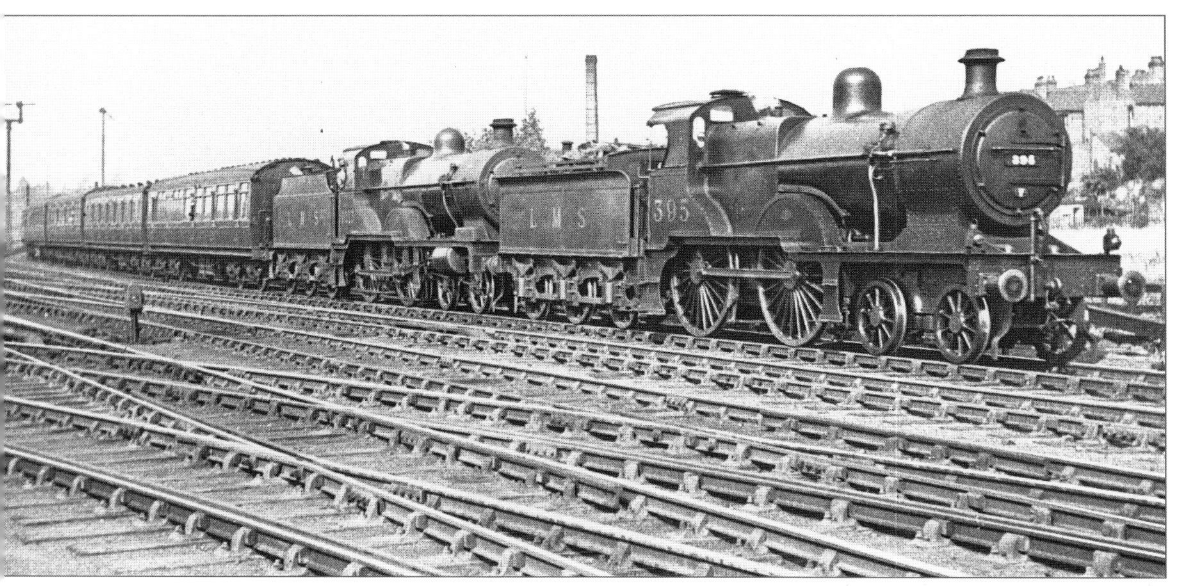

Ex MR 2P 4–4–0 LMS No. 395 piloting a three-cylinder Compound 4–4–0 on what is probably the 'Pines Express' to Bournmouth on the Midland Railway's Wolverhampton–Walsall line. The train will run to Birmingham (New Street) and then join the Somerset & Dorset Railway at Bath for the journey to the south-coast resort.

A pair of ex-Midland Railway 2P 4–4–0s, headed by loco No. 486, head south along the MR line to Walsall, 1920s.

LMS Stanier 2–6–2 tank No. 102 of Stafford shed at the head of a local train to Walsall on the MR line, early 1930s.

Ex-Midland 0–6–0 seen here as LMS No. 8088 at the head of a coal train on the Midland Railway line to Walsall 1920s.

CHAPTER FOUR

NATIONALISATION

Following the end of the Second World War, which saw the railways overused and undermaintained, a new Labour government was elected that had a policy of wholesale nationalisation of key industries, including the railways. Aware of the growth in private road competition, the government envisaged an integrated transport system and its 1947 Transport Act called for nationalisation of road haulage and the railways, which was to take effect from 1 January 1948. The 'Big Four' railway companies were to cease to exist at midnight on 31 December 1947.

Following implementation of the Transport Act, the railway system at Wolverhampton became part of the new British Railways. High Level was no longer owned by the LMS and came under the control of the London-Midland Region, while Low Level became part of the Western Region. As the oldest remaining railway company, and having retained its original title, the GWR ceased to exist after nearly a century at Wolverhampton. Neither of the two stations had suffered damage during the war and they passed into public ownership intact. For several years it appeared that nothing had changed at Low Level as ex-GWR locos retained their cast-brass cabside number plates and four digit numbers. Only cast smokebox numberplates and the 'Lion and Wheel' corporate emblem on tender sides and tanks indicated a change of ownership. Ex-LMS locos, on the other hand, were eventually given numbers in the 40,000 and 50,000 series after nationalisation as well as having their express locos painted in GWR Brunswick Green instead of LMS Crimson Lake, which was a much clearer sign of new ownership.

As the system settled into BR ownership, a new 'golden age' for the railways dawned as the 1950s arrived. This was the period of full employment and paid holidays as a postwar boom in manufacturing brought about increasing prosperity for the working people of Britain. During this period, many families enjoyed seaside holidays for the first time and they looked to the railways to provide rapid transport to holiday destinations. Summer traffic of this kind reached a peak in 1957, private motor cars and motor coaches taking an increasing share of this traffic, although by no means all of it, after that glorious summer. At Wolverhampton there were excursions and extra trains to West Country resorts and the Cambrian coast from Low Level, while trains to the North Wales coast, north-west of England resorts and Scotland operated from High Level station.

From the early 1950s, new trains were introduced between Wolverhampton and London. On 15 September 1950, LM Region introduced 'The Midlander' restaurant-car service from High Level to Euston, covering the distance to Euston in 2 hours

40 minutes. Ex-LMS rebuilt 'Royal-Scot' 4–6–0 No. 46140 *The King's Royal Rifle Corps* had the honour of hauling the first of these trains. Down at Low Level, WR introduced 'The Inter City', a 'King'-hauled express operating between Wolverhampton and Paddington. In 1951, the Paddington–Aberystwyth, via Low Level, train was introduced in 1951 as 'The Cambrian Coast Express'. In the late 1950s, the regions were given some freedom to take a more individual course, WR introduced Mk 1 coaches in the old GWR chocolate and cream livery for its express trains, and both 'The Inter City' and 'Cambrian Coast Express' were provided with these coaches.

Modernisation of the railways at Wolverhampton, which began with the introduction of DMU sets on local trains, was to bring about a major transformation to the network in the town, and a great deal of the old system was to disappear during the 1960s.

Some Named Trains that Called at Wolverhampton

1955

'The Cambrian Coast Express'	Paddington–Aberystwyth and Pwllheli
'The Cornishman'	Wolverhampton (L.L.)–Penzance and Kingswear
'The Inter-City'	Paddington–Wolverhampton (L.L.)
'The Midlander'	Wolverhampton (H.L.)–Euston

1991

'The Midland Scot'	Glasgow–Birmingham (New Street)
'The Clansman'	Euston–Inverness
'The Devon Scot'	Edinburgh–Plymouth
'The Cornish Scot'	Glasgow–Penzance
'The Sussex Scot'	Glasgow–Brighton
'The Wessex Scot'	Glasgow–Poole
'The Dorset Scot'	Edinburgh–Poole
'The Birmingham Pullman'	Euston–Wolverhampton

Wolverhampton (High Level) station looking towards Birmingham with goods sidings off to the left in BR days. The overall roof looks a little the worse for wear. Note that the name totem is still lit by gas, a form of lighting that had persisted since LNWR days and which would only be replaced with electric lighting when the station was rebuilt.

High Level station with a train for Birmingham leaving at the far end. There appears to be plenty of parcels traffic judging by the number of bags on both platforms and, on the middle right, a consignment of new bicycles appear to have been delivered.

High Level station not long before the station was closed for rebuilding, 1960s. When the old station was demolished, the contractors found a honeycomb of rooms underneath the platform; the purpose of these was never clearly understood.

High Level station looking towards Stafford with a DMU approaching, early 1960s. Wolverhampton No. 3 signal-box is visible adjacent to a rake of coaches at the buffer stops and the ex-LMS carriage shed is in the background. On the extreme left, a parcels van is being loaded.

The Birmingham end of High Level station with goods wagons at Mill Street goods depot on the right. LMS Class 3F 0–6–0 'Jinty' tank loco, the Mill Street shunter, just past the signal-box is at rest. The signal-box is Wolverhampton No. 2 and there is an array of ex-LMS semaphore signals.

An unidentified ex-LMS Stanier 'Black 5' 4–6–0 leaving High Level with a train for Birmingham (New Street). In view are goods avoiding lines at High Level and the frontage of the ex-GWR Low Level station. On the extreme right, an ex-GWR 0–6–0 pannier tank is on an empty stock train and the former GWR carriage shed is in the background. This view was taken from the Jones's Mill roof.

Table 12

Table 12

THE MIDLANDER

REFRESHMENT CAR EXPRESS

LONDON, BIRMINGHAM and WOLVERHAMPTON

WEEK DAYS
(Mondays to Fridays)

		am
Wolverhampton (High Level)	dep	11D 0
Birmingham (New Street)	„	11D30
Coventry	„	11D56
		pm
London (Euston)	arr	1 30

		pm
London (Euston)	dep	5A50
Coventry	arr	7 24
Birmingham (New Street)	„	7 50
Bescot	„	8 14
Wolverhampton (High Level)	„	8 30

A—Seats can be reserved in advance on payment of a fee of 1s. 0d. per seat (see page 26).

D—Except for 26th July, 1st, 2nd, 5th, 6th and 9th August, seats can be reserved in advance on payment of a fee of 1s. 0d. per seat (see page 26).

59

A timetable for 'The Midlander' express which ran from High Level to London (Euston), *c*. 1958.

Ex-LMS rebuilt 'Royal Scot' 4–6–0 No. 46130 *The West Yorkshire Regiment* in BR green livery passes Wolverhampton No. 4 signal-box as it enters the town with a southbound ten-coach train at 3.40 p.m., 30 June 1951. The ex-LMS carriage shed is just behind the train.

The unthinkable – GWR train on LNWR metals! Captain Huish would have had apoplexy if he'd seen it. This situation arose because a Sunday diversion, owing to repairs on Shifnal bridge (on the S&B line), rerouted the train via Wellington, Stafford and Bushbury and reached Low Level via Commercial Road on 29 November 1953. The train is ex-GWR Collett 'Castle' class 4–6–0 No. 5015 *Kingswear Castle* at the head of a Paddington-bound express. Bushbury Down sidings are on the left and Bushbury loco shed is on the right.

Ex-LMS 'Patriot' class 4–6–0 No. 45539 *E.C. Trench* with high-sided Stanier tender, which had been paired with the loco the previous May, is seen passing Fordhouses siding with a southbound express, 5 August 1956. The train had been brought to a stand at the south end of the sidings. This locomotive had been allocated to Longsight shed, Manchester, and was transferred to Liverpool Edge Hill shed in October 1956.

Ex-LMS Fowler 3P 2–6–2 tank loco No. 40066, minus smokebox number plate, is returning to Wolverhampton (High Level) with a Euston inspectors' saloon after visiting burnt-out carriage No. 27058, 21 March 1952. The inspectors did not use a proper saloon but a coach of the same batch as the one that caught fire. The incident occurred between Sutton Coldfield and Wolverhampton on the ex-Midland line. This coach was attached to the Euston Wolverhampton (High Level) train for the visit.

Ex-LMS Fowler 2–6–2 tank loco running round the inspectors' coach at Fordhouses, 21 March 1952. It has just brought the Euston inspectors to view the burnt-out coach M27058.

Burnt-out coach No. 27058 with tarpaulins removed for inspection, at the north end of Fordhouses sidings, 21 March 1952. The coach has the 'blood and custard' livery used by BR at that time.

Lady Godiva with clothes on! LMS 'Patriot' class 4–6–0 No. 5519 *Lady Godiva* at the north end of Bushbury sidings, just north of Bee Lane Bridge, covered in a tarpaulin after becoming derailed, 27 April 1947.

Inspection saloon No. 45010 attached to the rear of the 9.20 a.m. ex-Crewe express at High Level station.

The burnt-out wreckage of an ex-LNWR goods brake van No. M281147, 25 March 1951. The view was taken at Bushbury, from Bushbury Lane bridge, looking towards Stafford.

A Brake Third Class open coach ex-LMS No. M9861M with BR 'blood and custard' livery at the north end of Fordhouses sidings, 29 April 1956. Carriages were handled at the old GWR goods yard at Oxley at this time.

The railway overbridge at Bushbury. Such was its narrow bore that it caused a road traffic bottleneck.

Ex-LNWR 2–4–2 No. 46701 tank loco (ex-Warrington) at Littles Lane Bridge is being prepared to collect its motor train and propel it into High Level station for the run to Walsall, 30 April 1952. It was pressed into service to replace ex-LMS 2–6–2 tank loco, which was then undergoing repair, on the ex-Midland Railway service to Walsall.

Ex-LNWR 2–4–2 No. 46701 tank loco propels its two-coach motor train into High Level station for the journey to Walsall.

Table 77 — BIRMINGHAM, MONUMENT LANE, BESCOT, WALSALL, and WOLVERHAMPTON

Week Days

Miles	Station	a.m	a.m	a.m	a.m	a.m	a.m	a.m	p.m	p.m	a.m	p.m	p.m	a.m.	a.m	p.m	p.m
	50 London (Euston) ...dep	..	..	..	..	..	..	..	..	S	8 55	S	S	10E28	1130	S	E
—	Birmingham (N. St.)...dep	5 55	..	6 33	7 37	8 35	..	9 45	..	..	1215	..	..	1 15	2 30	..	..
1½	Vauxhall and Duddeston...	5 58	..	6 36	7 40	..	..	9 48	..	12 9	1218	1240	..	1 18	2 33	..	..
2½	Aston	6 3	..	6 40	7 44	..	..	9 53	..	1212	1222	1243	..	1 22	2 37	..	..
3¼	Witton	6 7	..	6 44	7 47	..	..	9 56	..	1216	1225	1248	..	1 25	2 40	..	..
4¼	Perry Barr	6 11	..	6 47	7 50	..	..	9 59	..	1219	1228	1251	..	1 28	2 43	..	..
—	Monument Lane	..	..	..	..	8 39	..	..	..	..	..	..	..	..	..	..	..
—	Winson Green	..	..	..	..	..	..	..	..	..	..	..	..	..	..	..	..
5¾	Great Barr A	6 17	..	6 51	7 54	8 50	..	10 3	..	1223	1232	1255	1 9	1 32	2 47	..	..
7¼	Newton Road	..	..	..	..	..	..	..	..	..	..	..	..	..	..	..	..
9¼	Bescot	6 26	..	7 0	8 3	8 59	9 56	1013	..	1234	1243	1 5	1 19	1 43	2 57	..	..
11	Walsall arr	6 30	..	7 4	8 11	9 6	10 0	1017	..	1238	1247	1 9	1 23	1 47	3 1	..	..
	Walsall dep	..	7 2	..	8 20	9 12	..	..	1214	..	..	..	..	2 0	..	3 44	4 10
—	Pleck	..	7 4	..	8 22	9 14	..	..	1216	..	..	..	..	2 2	..	3 46	4 12
10¾	Darlaston	..	7 7	..	8 25	9 17	..	..	1219	..	..	..	..	2 5	..	3 49	4 16
12½	Willenhall (Bilston St.)...	..	7 13	..	8 29	9 21	..	..	1223	..	..	..	..	2 9	..	3 53	4 22
15½	Wolverhampton ......arr	..	7 22	..	8 40	9 30	..	..	1232	..	..	..	..	2 19	..	4 2	4 31

Miles	Station	p.m	p.m	p.m	p.m	p.m	p.m	p.m	p.m	pm	p.m	p.m	a.m	p.m		
	50 London (Euston) ...dep	..	2 20	E	S	..	..	..	4 25	..	..	5 35	6 55	6 55	E 7 5	S 7 5
—	Birmingham (N. St.)...dep	4 12	5 26	..	..	5 55	6 33	6 55	7 0	..	..	8 35	9 15	9 25	1035	1047
1½	Vauxhall and Duddeston...	4 15	..	5 35	..	5 58	6 36	7Y7	RC London to Wolverhampton	..	..	8 39	RC (except on Sats.) and RC from London (Eus.)	9 28	1038	1050
2½	Aston	4 19	..	5 38	..	6 4	6 40	7 12		..	..	8 43		9 32	1042	1054
3¼	Witton	4 22	..	5 47	..	6 9	6X47	7 19		..	..	8 46		..	..	..
4¼	Perry Barr	4 25	..	5 53	..	6 13	6 52	7K29		..	..	8 49		9 37	1047	1059
—	Monument Lane	..	..	..	..	..	..	..		..	..	..		..	..	..
—	Winson Green	..	..	..	..	..	..	..		..	..	..		..	..	..
5¾	Great Barr A	4 29	..	5 58	..	6 17	6 56	7 33		..	..	8 53		9 41	1051	11 3
7¼	Newton Road	..	..	..	..	..	..	..		..	..	..		..	..	..
9¼	Bescot	4 39	5 46	6 9	..	6 27	7 7	7 44	7 19	726	..	9 3		9 50	11 1	1112
11	Walsall arr	4 43	5 50	6 13	..	6 31	7 11	7 51	..	730	..	9 7		9 54	11 5	1116
	Walsall dep	5 24	..	..	6 17	6E35	..	..	..	..	8 17	..		10 2	..	..
—	Pleck	5 26	..	..	6 20	6E37	..	..	..	..	8 19	..		10 4	..	..
10¾	Darlaston	5 29	..	..	6 23	6E42	..	..	..	..	8 23	..		10 7	..	..
12½	Willenhall (Bilston St.)...	5 35	..	..	6 27	6E51	..	..	..	..	8 30	..		1011	..	..
15½	Wolverhampton ......arr	5 44	..	..	6 36	7 E1	..	..	7 31	..	8 39	..	9 42	1020	..	..

Week Days

Miles	Station	a.m	am	am	am	am	am	a.m	a.m	a.m	am	a.m	a.m	a.m	a.m	
	Wolverhampton ......dep	..	622	7 2	..	..	..	7 15	..	..	..	8 27	..	9 20	1057	..
3	Willenhall (Bilston St.)...	..	632	..	..	..	..	7 22	..	..	..	8 35	..	9 27	11 4	..
4½	Darlaston	..	636	..	..	..	..	7 26	..	..	..	8 39	..	9 33	11 8	..
—½	Pleck	..	639	..	..	..	..	7 29	..	..	..	8 42	..	..	1111	..
6¾	Walsall arr	..	644	..	..	..	..	7 34	..	..	..	8 46	..	..	1116	..
	Walsall dep	5 45	648	..	656	7 6	716	7 45	7 55	8 15	837	9 20	9 30	..	1210	..
6½	Bescot	5 50	654	..	7 2	712	722	7 50	7Z59	8 19	841	9 24	9 34	9 42	1215	..
7½	Newton Road	..	..	..	..	..	..	..	..	..	..	..	..	..	..	..
9½	Great Barr A	5 56	7 0	..	..	718	728	7 56	..	8 25	847	9 30	..	9 48	1221	..
—	Winson Green	..	..	..	..	..	..	..	..	8 35	..	..	..	..	..	..
—	Monument Lane	..	..	..	..	..	..	..	..	8 38	..	..	..	..	..	..
11½	Perry Barr	6 1	7 5	..	714	..	733	8 4	..	..	851	9 34	..	9 52	1225	..
12¼	Witton	6 5	712	..	720	..	740	8 9	..	..	856	..	..	9 55	1228	..
13	Aston	6 9	715	..	723	..	743	8 12	..	..	9 2	9 39	..	10 0	1231	..
14	Vauxhall & Duddeston....	6 14	721	..	..	..	748	8 16	..	..	9 6	9 43	..	10 4	1235	..
15½	Birmingham (N. St.)...arr	6 22	731	751	..	..	..	..	8 19	8 51	915	9 52	..	1011	1243	..
128	50 London (Euston) ....arr	..	..	..	100	..	..	..	1050	1225	..	1240	..	3 30	..	..

Miles	Station	p.m	p.m	p.m	p.m	p.m	p.m	p.m	p.m	p.m		p.m	p.m		p.m	p.m	p.m	p.m
	Wolverhampton ......dep	S	1 5	E	S	S	..	3 50	5 17	5 43	RC (except on Saturdays) and TC to London (Euston)	E	S	..	5 58	6 50	8 20	1010
3	Willenhall (Bilston St.)...	..	1 11	..	..	..	..	3 56	5 25	..		..	..	..	6 6	6 59	8 27	1017
4½	Darlaston	..	1 15	..	..	..	..	4 0	5 31	..		..	..	..	6 10	7 5	8 33	1021
—½	Pleck	..	1 20	..	..	..	..	4 4	5 34	..		..	..	..	6 13	7 8	8 36	1024
6¾	Walsall arr	..	1 26	..	..	..	..	4 9	5 39	..		..	..	..	6 18	7 13	8 41	1029
	Walsall dep	1240	..	1 40	1 45	2 30	3 14	4 15	5 42	..		6 15	6 17	..	..	7N23	9 39	..
6½	Bescot	1245	..	1 44	1 49	2 34	3 19	4 20	5 47	5 56		6 19	6 24	..	..	7 28	9 43	..
7½	Newton Road	..	..	..	..	..	..	..	..	..		..	..	..	..	..	..	..
9½	Great Barr A	1251	..	1 50	1 55	2 40	3 25	4 26	5 53	..		6 25	6 30	..	..	7 35	9 49	..
—	Winson Green	..	..	..	..	..	..	..	..	..		..	6 45	..	..	..	..	..
—	Monument Lane	..	..	..	..	2 53	..	..	..	..		..	6 48	..	..	..	..	..
11½	Perry Barr	1255	..	1 54	1 59	..	3 29	4 30	5 57	..		6 31	..	..	..	7 39	9 53	..
12¼	Witton	1258	..	1 57	2 2	..	3 32	4 33	6 4	..		6 35	..	..	..	7 43	..	..
13	Aston	1 2	..	2 0	2 5	..	3 35	4 36	6 7	..		6 38	..	..	..	7 47	9 58	..
14	Vauxhall & Duddeston....	1 6	..	2 4	2 9	..	3 39	4 40	6 13	..		6 42	..	..	..	7 51	10 6	..
15½	Birmingham (N. St.)...arr	1 15	..	2 13	2 20	3 1	3 51	4 51	6 25	6 13		..	6 56	..	..	7 59	1016	..
128	50 London (Euston) ....arr	..	..	4 50	4 50	5 50	7E0	7 50	..	8 40		..	1055	..	..	..	5J0	..

Sundays

Station	a.m.	p.m	a.m	p.m	p.m	p.m	p.m	
50 London (Euston) ...dep	..	..	1115	..	..	4 15	7 5	..
Birmingham (N.St.) ...dep	9 25	1245	2 30	4 33	5 50	7 30	1045	..
Vauxhall and Duddeston...	9 28	1248	2 33	4 36	5 53	7 33	1048	..
Aston	9 32	1252	2 37	4 40	5 57	7 37	1052	..
Witton	..	..	..	..	..	..	..	..
Perry Barr	9 37	1257	2 42	4 46	6 2	7 50	1057	..
Monument Lane	..	..	..	..	..	..	..	..
Winson Green	..	..	..	..	..	..	..	..
Great Barr A	9 41	1 1	2 46	4 50	6 6	7 54	11 1	..
Newton Road	..	..	..	..	..	..	..	..
Bescot	9 50	1 12	2 56	5 0	6 16	8 4	1110	..
Walsall arr	9 54	1 16	3 0	5 4	6 20	8 8	1114	..
Walsall dep	11 10	..	..	5 26	6 35	9 50	..	..
Pleck	..	..	..	..	..	..	..	..
Darlaston	..	..	..	..	..	..	..	..
Willenhall (Bilston St.)	..	..	..	..	..	..	..	..
Wolverhampton ......arr	11 26	..	..	5 42	6 51	10 6	..	..

Sundays

Station	a.m	a.m	p.m	p.m	p.m	p.m	p.m	p.m
Wolverhampton .. dep	..	11 7	1 28	..	..	6 8	..	1015
Willenhall (Bilston St.)	..	..	..	..	..	..	..	..
Darlaston	..	..	..	..	..	..	..	..
Pleck	..	..	..	..	..	..	..	..
Walsall arr	..	1123	1 44	..	..	6 24	..	1031
Walsall dep	9 5	1 30	..	3 10	4 10	7 20	9 32	..
Bescot	9 9	1 34	..	3 14	4 14	7 24	9 36	..
Newton Road	..	..	..	..	..	..	..	..
Great Barr A	9 15	1 40	..	3 20	4 20	7 32	9 42	..
Winson Green	..	..	..	..	..	..	..	..
Monument Lane	..	..		..	..	..	..	..
Perry Barr	9 19						9 46	..
Witton	..							..
Aston	9 24							
Vauxhall & Duddeston	9 28							
Birmingham (N.St.) arr	9 36							
50 London (Euston) arr	1 30	5 10						

A Sta. for Hamstead (2 miles from Great Barr)
E or E Except Sats.
J Sunday mornings only
K Arr. 7 23 p.m
N 2 minutes later on Saturdays
RC Restaurant Car
S or S Sats. only
TC Thro' Carriages
X Arr. 6 44 p.m
Y Arr. 7 1 p.m
Z Stops to take up only

OTHER TRAINS

BETWEEN	TABLE
Birmingham and Winson Green ..	76
Birmingham and Walsall	262
Birmingham and Wolverhampton	76

A 1947 timetable for the service from Wolverhampton (High Level) to Walsall, as well as to Birmingham.

Ex-LMS and Midland Railway 2P 4–4–0. 40692, paired with an ex-Lancashire & Yorkshire Railway inspection saloon, No. M45039M, at the ex-MR Wednesfield station, 10 July 1958. The saloon was the Northampton District Engineer's and was on loan to Walsall while theirs was undergoing repair. The view is looking towards Wolverhampton.

Ex-LNWR 'Super D' 0–8–0 No. 49328 near the former MR goods yard at Wednesfield Road. The loco is hauling a goods train to Oxley. On the left is an ex-GWR rail motor coach.

BR 'Standard' class 4 2–6–0 No. 76039 on shunting duties inside the former Midland Railway goods yard at Wednesfield Road, 21 October 1965. Following nationalisation, BR remained committed to steam traction and built a series of two-cylinder 'Standard' locomotives in an effort to meet its traffic needs and allow some old pre-grouping engines to be withdrawn. The first of these new 'Standards' to be introduced was No. 70000 *Britannia*, a two-cylinder Pacific loco built at Crewe in 1951. The 'Standard' class 4s were introduced in 1953 and continued to be built until 1957. Among the loco and yard staff is Mr Winwood (loco driver) of Rose Cottage, Duck Lane, Bilbrook.

Ex-LNWR 'Super D' 0–8–0 No. 48895 enters the ex-MR yard at Wednesfield Road, October 1960.

Fowler 4F 0–6–0 No. 43940 entering the ex-MR Wednesfield Road with an ex-Water Orton goods train 13 February 1964. This was very much a Midland engine and at home in this yard. It was one of a class of 192 engines built in the Midland Railway works at Derby between 1911 and 1922 and designed by Henry Fowler. The LMS went on to build another 772 locos of this type.

Another ex-Midland Railway loco, class 2 0–6–0 No. 58152, built to a Johnson design of 1875, at Wednesfield Road goods yard, 19 September 1952. The locomotive was allocated to Bushbury shed. This class of engines survived for a long time and the last, No. 58182, was not withdrawn until January 1964; it was then the oldest engine on the British railway network, having been built in 1876.

EXPRESS AND STAR, TUESDAY, OCTOBER 29, 1963 5

TRANSPORT ACT 1962

Withdrawal of Railway Passenger Services

The London Midland Railway Board hereby gives notice, in accordance with Section 56(7) of the Transport Act 1962, that on and from 6th JANUARY, 1964, they propose to discontinue all railway passenger services between

WOLVERHAMPTON HIGH LEVEL, WALSALL, LICHFIELD CITY and BURTON-ON-TRENT

and from the following stations:—

Willenhall Bilston Street	**Hammerwich**
Darlaston	**Lichfield Trent Valley High Level**
Pelsall	
Brownhills	**Alrewas**

It appears to the Board that the following alternative services will be available:—

BY RAIL

Between Wolverhampton and Lichfield, and between Wolverhampton and Burton-on-Trent, via Birmingham New Street.

BY ROAD

Route No.	Service
Wolverhampton Corporation Transport	
5	Wolverhampton - Willenhall
29	Wolverhampton - Willenhall - Walsall
42	Wolverhampton - Willenhall - New Invention
Walsall Corporation Transport	
4	Walsall - Pelsall - Brownhills - Heath Hayes
9	Walsall - Walsall Wood - Shenstone - Wall
11	Walsall - Pelsall - Brownhills
12	Walsall - Pelsall - Bloxwich
16	Walsall - Pipe Hill - Lichfield
17	Walsall - Pelsall - Norton - Heath Hayes - Cannock - Cheslyn Hay
19	Walsall - Pelsall - Brownhills - Chasetown - Burntwood
23	Walsall - Brownhills
29	Walsall - Willenhall - Wolverhampton
37	Walsall - Wednesbury - Darlaston - Walsall
38	Walsall - Darlaston - Wednesbury - Walsall
41	Walsall - New Invention - Willenhall
44	Boney Hay - Chase Terrace - Burntwood - Pipe Hill - Lichfield
45	Beaudesert - Burntwood - Hammerwich - Lichfield
46	Goosemoor Green - Burntwood - Lichfield
47	Cannock - Heath Hayes - Chasetown - Burntwood - Lichfield
48	Walsall - Rushall - High Heath (Pelsall)
62	Brownhills - Hammerwich - Lichfield
Harper Bros. (Heath Hayes) Ltd.	
Cannock	Cannock - Heath Hayes
Kingstanding	Brownhills - Aldridge - Kingstanding
Lichfield	Lichfield - Wall - Stonnall
Kingstanding	Aldridge - Kingstanding
Birmingham & Midland Motor Omnibus Co. Ltd.	
X12	Birmingham - Lichfield - Burton-on-Trent - Derby
104	Birmingham - Sutton Coldfield - Streetly - Brownhills - Cannock
112	Birmingham - Lichfield - Alrewas - Burton-on-Trent
277	Willenhall - Darlaston

Any user of the rail services it is proposed to withdraw, and any body representing such users desirous of objecting to the proposal, may lodge objections within six weeks of 8th NOVEMBER, 1963, i.e., not later than 21st DECEMBER, 1963, addressing the objections to:—

The Secretary of the Transport Users' Consultative Committee for the West Midlands, 29, Smallbrook, Ringway, Birmingham, 5

NOTE.—If any objections are lodged within the period specified above the closure cannot be proceeded with until the Transport Users' Consultative Committee has reported to the Minister and the Minister has given his consent (Section 56 (8) of the Transport Act, 1962).

An ominous sign of things to come. An announcement in the *Wolverhampton Express and Star* of the closure of the ex-MR line from Wolverhampton to Walsall and its replacement with bus services.

An unidentified ex-GWR Collett 'King' Class 4–6–0 is seen leaving Wolverhampton (Low Level) station and heading towards Birmingham (Snow Hill) with a Paddington express, late 1950s. On the right are the lines to Heath Town Junction.

Just beyond the south end of Low Level station are the tunnels that trains pass under to gain access to the BW&D line to Birmingham (Snow Hill). On the left are tracks that connect with the MR line at Heath Town Junction. On the embankment is ex-LNWR Wolverhampton No. 1 signal-box and a relief line on an arch above the tunnels can also be seen. In the siding on the right is an ex-GWR rail motor coach painted in BR maroon.

South of Low Level station is an unidentified ex-GWR 4–6–0 and an ex-LMS Reid composite coach. The bars across the droplights suggest it was used on the Maryport and Carlisle line in Cumbria; it is certainly a long way from home.

Ex-GWR Churchward 2–6–0 No. 6340 is leaving Low Level station with an up parcels train, 1955. The ex-GWR carriage shed can be seen in the background.

Ex-GWR Churchward 2–6–0 No. 6340 south of Low Level station on stock marshalling duties.

SUMMARY TABLES **Table 27**

Table 27

LONDON (Euston and Paddington) AND BIRMINGHAM (New St. and Snow Hill) AND WOLVERHAMPTON (High Level and Low Level)

WEEK DAYS

					RS	RS	R	K	E	L	R	R	RS	S	E	R	
	a.m.	a.m.	a.m.	a.m.	a.m	a.m.	a.m.	a.m.	a.m.	a.m.	a.m.	a.m.	a.m.	a.m.	a.m.	p.m.	p.m.
LONDON (Euston) ....dep.	12 2	...	6 45	...	8 55	...	...	...	...	...	10 20	...	11 25	...	...	1 22	...
" (Paddington) .... "	...	12 5	...	7 5	...	9 0	9 10	10 10	10 10	10 10	...	11 10	...	11 45	11 45	...	2 10
Birmingham (New St.)........arr.	3 2	...	10 24	...	11 30	...	...	...	...	...	12a55	...	1 55	...	...	4 14	...
" (Snow Hill)...... "	...	3 56	...	10 29	...	11 15	11 50	12 30	12 30	12 30	...	1 37	...	2 48	3 23	...	4 37
Wolverhampton (H.L.)........ "	3 48	...	11 29	...	11 57	...	...	...	...	...	2 12	...	2 30	...	...	...	...
" (L.L.)........ "	...	4 30	...	10 55	...	11 40	12 15	12 53	1 29	1 35	...	2 2	...	3 12	3 46	...	5 2

WEEK DAYS—*continued*

	BS	B	RS	E	RS	R	RS									
	p.m.	p.m.	p.m.	p.m.	p.m.	p.m.	p.m.	p.m.		p.m.		p.m.		ngt.	ngt.	
LONDON (Euston) ....dep.	2 15	...	4 30	R	5 35	...	6 55	7 5	...	...	...	9 35	...	12 2	...	...
" (Paddington) .... "	...	4 10	...	5 10	...	6 10	...	...	...	7 35	...	...	...	...	12 5	...
Birmingham (New St.)........arr.	4 35	...	7 0	...	8 0	...	9 15	10 20	...	...	...	12 40	...	3‡2	...	...
" (Snow Hill)...... "	...	6 46	...	7 38	...	8 49	...	...	...	11 5	..	...	...	...	3 56	...
Wolverhampton (H.L.)........ "	5 6	...	7 31	...	8 30	...	9 43	11 35	...	...	...	...	...	3‡48	...	...
" (L.L.)........ "	...	7 11	...	8 0	...	9 15	...	...	...	11 40	...	...	...	...	4 30	...

SUNDAYS

				R												
	a.m.	a.m.	a.m.	a.m.	a.m.	p.m.	p.m.	p.m.		p.m.	p.m.	p.m.	p.m.	ngt.	ngt.	
LONDON (Euston) ....dep.	12 2	...	...	...	11 15	...	4 30	...	...	6 55	7 5	...	8 53	12 2	...	...
" (Paddington) .... "	...	12 5	10 10	11 10	...	4 0	...	6 10	...	...	...	8 10	...	...	12 5	...
Birmingham (New St.)........arr.	3 8	...	...	...	2 20	...	7 20	...	...	9 20	10 20	...	12 20	3 2	...	...
" (Snow Hill)...... "	...	3 56	1 23	1 40	...	7 21	...	8 53	...	...	...	11 40	...	...	3 56	...
Wolverhampton (H.L.)........ "	3 52	...	...	...	2 55	...	7 50	...	...	10 36	11 2	a.m.	...	3 48	...	...
" (L.L.)........ "	...	4 30	...	2 8	...	7 57	...	9 19	...	...	...	12 5	...	...	4 30	...

WEEK DAYS

	M	H			RS	E	S	RS		B		BS	R	R	RS	S
	a.m.	a.m.		a.m.	a.m.	a.m.	a.m.	a.m.	a.m.	a.m.	a.m.	a.m.	a.m.	a.m.	p.m.	p.m.
Wolverhampton (L.L.)........dep.	...	...	...	6 45	...	7 10	...	...	...	8 33	9 35	...	10 20	11 34	...	12 46
" (H.L.) .... "	...	...	...	...	6 40	...	7 22	8 0	...	...	...	9 40	...	...	12 5	...
Birmingham (Snow Hill) ...... "	...	12 44	...	7 20	...	8 0	...	...	...	9 0	10 0	...	10 45	12 0	...	1 12
" (New St.)........ "	12 20	...	...	...	7 30	...	8 25	8 40	8 45	...	...	10 15	...	...	12 40	...
LONDON (Paddington) ....arr.	...	5 35	...	10 5	...	10 15	...	...	...	11 20	12 25	...	2 15	2 35	...	3 20
" (Euston) .... "	3 25	...	...	...	10 10	...	10 55	11 0	11 25	...	...	12 50	...	...	3 0	...

WEEK DAYS—*continued*

	J	RS	R	R	RS	E	E	S	RS	R	R			S		
	p.m.	p.m.	p.m.	p.m.	p.m.	p.m.	p.m.	p.m.	p.m.	p.m.	p.m.	p.m.	p.m.	p.m.		p.m.
Wolverhampton (L.L.)........dep.	1 10	...	2 40	...	...	R	...	...	4 20	...	5 33	...	7 25	...	...	11 45
" (H.L. .... "	...	1 55	...	...	3 3	4 5	...	4 5	...	...	...	6 30	...	10 43	...	a.m.
Birmingham (Snow Hill ...... "	1 35	...	3 5	...	...	...	...	...	4 45	...	6 0	...	7 50	...	...	12 44
" (New St.)........ "	...	2 30	...	2 50	4 0	4 45	5 0	5 0	...	5 23	...	7 40	...	...	...	...
LONDON (Paddington) ....arr.	4 10	...	5 40	...	...	...	...	...	7 5	...	8 40	...	10 10	a.m.	...	5 35
" (Euston) .... "	...	4 55	...	5 55	6 40	7 5	7 50	7 50	...	8F25	...	10T55	...	5 10	...	...

SUNDAYS

										R		R				
	a.m.	a.m.	a.m.	a.m.		p.m.		p.m.	p.m.	p.m.		p.m.	p.m.	p.m.	p.m.	
Wolverhampton (L.L.)........dep.	...	...	...	11 15	...	...	...	...	4 40	...	...	6 10	...	7 55	...	...
" (H.L.) .... "	...	...	9 50	...	...	1 55	...	4 15	...	4 30	...	...	5V36	...	9 57	...
Birmingham (Snow Hill) ...... "	...	12 44	...	11 50	...	...	...	...	5 10	...	...	6 35	...	8 20	...	...
" (New St.)........ "	12 20	...	10 35	...	...	2 35	...	5 0	...	5 30	...	...	7 55	...	...	...
LONDON (Paddington) ....arr	...	5 35	...	2 20	...	...	...	...	7 50	...	...	9 20	...	11 40	a.m.	...
" (Euston) .... "	5 10	...	1 35	...	...	5 15	...	7 50	...	8 50	...	...	10 55	...	3 25	...

a On Saturdays arrive 1 5 p.m.
B Buffet Car whole or part of journey
BS Buffet Car, except on Saturdays
E Except Saturdays
F On Fridays arrive 8 35 p.m.
H Mondays excepted
J Saturdays only, and runs 9th July to 17th September, inclusive.
K Saturdays only and runs 2nd July to 10th September inclusive
L Saturdays only and runs to 25th June inclusive and commencing 17th September
M Mondays only
R Restaurant Car whole or part of journey
RS Restaurant Car, except on Saturdays
S Saturdays only
T On Saturdays arr. London (Euston) 11 0 p.m.
V Depart Wolverhampton (H.L.) 5.55 p.m. commencing 19th June.
‡ On Sunday mornings arrive Birmingham (New Street) 3 8 a.m., Wolverhampton (H.L.) 3 52 a.m.

Heavy figures indicate Through Carriages from or to London.

17

A composite timetable for services to London Paddington and Euston from both High and Low Level stations in the summer of 1949.

Table 13

Table 13

CAMBRIAN COAST EXPRESS

LONDON, ABERDOVEY, TOWYN, BARMOUTH, PWLLHELI and ABERYSTWYTH

WEEK DAYS

		R E	R S
		am	am
London (Paddington)	..dep	10A10	10A50
			pm
Banbury General ..	arr	11 20	12 11
	dep	11 22	12 15
Leamington Spa General	arr	..	12 39
	dep	..	12 43
		pm	
Birmingham (Snow Hill)	arr	12 13	1 15
	dep	12 17	1 20
Wolverhampton (Low Level)	arr	12 37	1 39
	dep	12 44	1 46
Shrewsbury	arr	1 19	..
	dep	1 23	..
Welshpool	..arr	2 1	2 56
Newtown	"	2 30	3 28
Machynlleth	"	3 17	4 18
Machynlleth ..	..dep	3 40	4 30
Penhelig Halt ..	..arr	4 4	4 51
Aberdovey	"	4 10	4 56
Towyn	"	4 19	5 3
Llwyngwril	"	4 36	5 15
Fairbourne	"	4 46	5 24
Barmouth Junction ..	"	4 50	5 27
Barmouth	"	4 57	5 33
Harlech	"	5 30	6 0
Portmadoc..	"	5 54	6 21
Criccieth	"	6 10	6 35
Pwllheli	"	6 26	7 0
Machynlleth	..dep	3 22	4 23
Borth	..arr	3 45	4 46
Aberystwyth	"	4 5	5 10

		R S	R E
		am	am
Aberystwyth ..	..dep	9A25	11A15
Borth	"	9A45	11A38
Dovey Junction ..	..arr	10 0	11 57
Pwllheli	..dep	..	9A30
Criccieth	"	..	9A48
Portmadoc	"	..	10A 0
Harlech	"	..	10A22
Barmouth	"	..	10A55
Barmouth Junction..	"	8A45	11A 1
Fairbourne	"	8A50	11A 5
Llwyngwril	"	9A 5	11A14
Tonfanau	"	9 15	11 24
Towyn	"	9A22	11A32
Aberdovey	"	9A30	11A39
Penhelig Halt	"	9 36	11 43
Dovey Junction	..arr	9 50	11 55
			pm
Dovey Junction ..	..dep	10A 8	12A 5
Machynlleth	"	10A20	12A16
Newtown	"	11 17	1 24
Welshpool	"	11 55	1 58
Shrewsbury	arr	..	2 37
	dep	..	2 41
		pm	
Wolverhampton (Low Level)	arr	1 11	3 28
	dep	1 18	3 35
Birmingham (Snow Hill)	arr	1 38	3 55
	dep	1 42	4 0
Leamington Spa General	arr	2 11	4 23
	dep	2 13	4 25
London (Paddington)	..arr	4 10	6 7

A—Seats can be reserved in advance on payment of a fee of 1s. 0d. per seat (see page 26).
E—Except Saturdays
R—Refreshment Car facilities between Paddington and Aberystwyth
S—Saturdays only

60

A 1958 timetable for the WR's 'Cambrian Coast Express' which ran between Paddington and Aberystwyth/Pwllheli in Mid and North Wales via Birmingham (Snow Hill), Wolverhampton (Low Level) and Shrewsbury.

Table 11

Table 11

THE INTER-CITY

REFRESHMENT CAR EXPRESS

LONDON, BIRMINGHAM and WOLVERHAMPTON

WEEK DAYS
(Mondays to Fridays)

Station		am
London (Paddington)	dep	9 A 0
High Wycombe	„	9K31
Birmingham (Snow Hill)	arr	11 7
Wolverhampton (Low Level)	„	11 30

Station		pm
Wolverhampton (Low Level)	dep	4B35
Birmingham (Snow Hill)	„	5 B 0
Leamington Spa General	„	5 26
High Wycombe	arr	6V41
London (Paddington)	„	7 15

A—Seats can be reserved in advance on payment of a fee of 1s. 0d. per seat (see page 26).

B—Except for 26th July and 2nd August, seats can be reserved in advance on payment of a fee of 1s. 0d. per seat (see page 26).

K—Calls to pick up passengers only.

V—Calls to set down passengers only.

A timetable for 'The Inter-City', an express introduced by WR to compete with LMR's 'The Midlander', 1958. This service ran from Low Level to Paddington via Birmingham (Snow Hill).

Table 14

Table 14

THE CORNISHMAN

REFRESHMENT CAR SERVICE

BETWEEN

WOLVERHAMPTON, BIRMINGHAM, GLOUCESTER, BRISTOL

AND THE

WEST OF ENGLAND

Via Stratford-upon-Avon

WEEK DAYS (Mondays to Fridays)

(For Services on Saturdays, see Table 33)

Station		am
WOLVERHAMPTON (Low Level)	dep	9 A 0
Bilston Central..	„	9 A 6
Wednesbury Central	„	9A12
West Bromwich	„	9A20
Birmingham (Snow Hill)	„	9A40
Stratford-upon-Avon	„	10 19
Cheltenham Spa (Malvern Road)	„	11 2
Gloucester Eastgate	„	11 20
		pm
Bristol (Temple Meads)	arr	12 15
Taunton	„	1 15
Exeter (St. David's)	„	1 58
Dawlish	„	2 33
Teignmouth	„	2 41
Newton Abbot	„	2 51
Torre	arr	3 8
Torquay	„	3 11
Paignton	„	3 21
Goodrington Sands Halt ..	„	3 24
Churston (for Brixham) ..	„	3 30
Kingswear	„	3 41
Plymouth (North Road)	arr	3 20
Liskeard	„	3 59
Bodmin Road	„	4 15
Par	„	4 28
St. Austell	„	4 39
Truro	„	5 2
St. Erth	„	5 38
Penzance	„	5 50

Station		am
PENZANCE	dep	10A30
St. Erth	„	10A40
Truro	„	11A20
St. Austell..	„	11 48
Par	„	11 57
		pm
Plymouth (North Road)..	„	1 0
Kingswear	dep	12A15
Churston (for Brixham) ..	„	12A30
Goodrington Sands Halt ..	„	12 40
Paignton	„	12A55
Torquay	„	1 A 2
Torre	„	1 7
Kingskerswell	„	1 15
Newton Abbot	dep	1 23
Teignmouth	„	1 34
Dawlish	„	1 42
Exeter (St. David's)..	„	2 24
Taunton	„	3 5
Bristol (Temple Meads)	„	4 8
Gloucester Eastgate	arr	5 3
Cheltenham Spa (Malvern Road)	„	5 21
Stratford-upon-Avon	„	6 3
Birmingham (Snow Hill).. ..	„	6 49
West Bromwich	„	7 4
Wednesbury Central	„	7 12
Bilston Central	„	7 18
Wolverhampton (Low Level)	„	7 25

A—Seats can be reserved in advance on payment of a fee of 1s. 0d. per seat (see page 26).

A timetable for WR's 'The Cornishman', West of England express, 1958. This train started at Low Level and ran via Birmingham (Snow Hill), then along the Birmingham & North Warwickshire Railway to Stratford-upon-Avon and on to Cheltenham, Gloucester and Bristol Temple Meads. It gained access to Bristol over ex-MR metals before joining the GWR main line from Paddington for the remainder of the journey to Penzance. This train was the one to be transferred to the Birmingham (New Street) and ex-MR line to Bristol in the 1960s when the GWR line at Low Level was threatened with closure.

Ex-GWR Collett 'Castle' class 4–6–0 No. 5065 *Newport Castle* waits at Low Level station with a southbound express, late 1950s. The engine is paired with a flat-sided Hawksworth tender instead of the usual Collett one. The coaches are finished in the 'blood and custard' livery favoured by BR at this time.

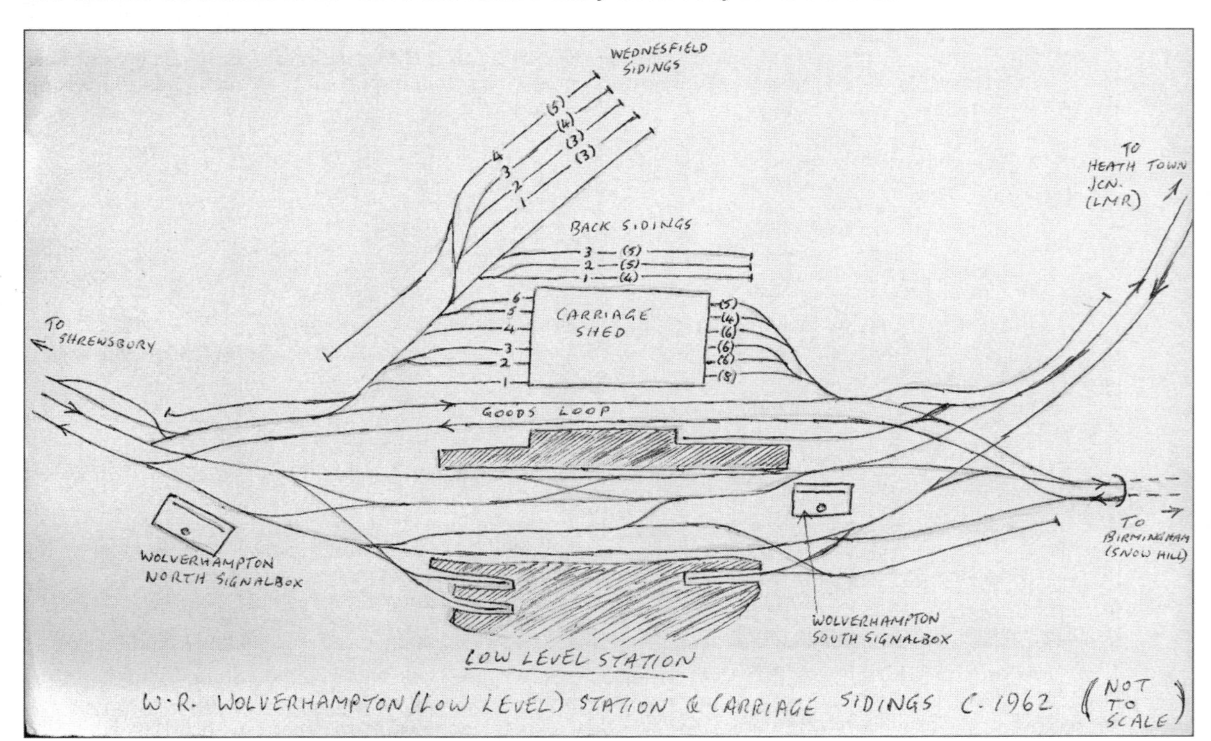

A plan of Low Level station, early 1960s. It shows the track plan inside the station, the carriage shed and sidings as well as the line to Shrewsbury and to Heath Town.

Looking down the chimney of ex-GWR Collett 'King' class 4–6–0 No. 6016 *King Edward V* in the sidings at Low Level, 1959. The loco has probably just brought in an express from Paddington and, as such, has the wrong headcode for a light engine.

Low Level station with an ex-GWR Churchward 2–6–2 Prairie tank No. 3102 of Stafford Road shed in the bay, late 1950s. The loco has probably brought in empty stock for a Paddington, via Worcester, train because it was unusual to see one of these engines in the bay. On the right is another ex-GWR loco on the goods bypass line with the carriage shed just visible on the extreme right.

Celebrating the centenary of the BW&D line, ex-GWR 0–4–2 tank loco No. 1438 is at the head of an SLS special from Low Level to Birmingham (Snow Hill), 13 November 1954.

The tender of ex-GWR Collett 'Manor' class 4–6–0 No. 7821 *Ditcheat Manor* at Low Level station, 1956. The original BR 'lion and wheel' emblem can be clearly seen. These 'Manor' class locos were a common sight at the head of the 'Cambrian Coast Express' from Shrewsbury to Aberystwyth. They replaced 'Castle' or 'King' class engines at Shrewsbury because they had the light axle loading required on the Cambrian coast route.

An ex-GWR side-corridor coach with 'American Bogies' at Low Level station, 1960. The coach was built in 1913.

Wolverhampton GWR Engineer's saloon No. 14643 at Cannock Road sidings, 27 May 1952.

Ex-GWR inspection saloon in chocolate and cream livery at Low Level, 20 October 1959. It is close to the carriage shed, out of sight, where it was normally kept.

Stafford Road shed, 15 June 1957. In the centre is a new three-car DMU set and a rake of ex-GWR coaches on the left. The Birmingham Canal is to the right. This was the point where the GWR line from Low Level met the S&B line to Shrewsbury.

Ex-LMS three-cylinder 4–4–0 Compound loco No. 41123 passes Oxley with the Talyllyn special for Mid Wales on its way to Shrewsbury over S&B metals, 1956. The expansive Oxley sidings are on the left and filled with a variety of tank wagons, open trucks and vans. Just to the left of the rake of wagons is Oxley North signal-box.

An unidentified ex-GWR 0–6–0 pannier tank and an ex-War Department 2–8–0 are running light engines towards Oxley near Birches Bridge, Codsall on the old Shrewsbury and Birmingham main line.

CHAPTER FIVE

THE LOCO SHEDS

If ever there was need for proof that Wolverhampton was principally a GWR town, despite the efforts of Mark Huish and the LNWR, it was the fact that the company had not one but two loco sheds in the town, at Stafford Road and Oxley. Their bitter rivals, the LNWR, had only a small shed at Bushbury.

Stafford Road shed was the older of the two, its origins dating back to 1854 when the GWR first reached Wolverhampton. At this time the company opened a broad gauge depot opposite a shed belonging to the Shrewsbury & Birmingham Railway, the two being separated by Stafford Road itself. After the amalgamation of the narrow gauge S&B and the GWR the latter realised that there was little hope of broad-gauge track ever going north of Wolverhampton and it seemed likely that the main line to Paddington would become narrow gauge in the very near future. The company, therefore, built a narrow gauge roundhouse in 1860. By 1875 two roundhouse sheds were added side by side, making three in all and providing sixty-one roads and a total area of 200 ft by 450 ft. These three sheds were originally of brick with slate roofs on timber trusses but were later reroofed in corrugated iron. The old broad-gauge depot was converted to a tender shop at the same time and the old S&B depot became an erecting shop. A two-road depot was constructed nearby to be superseded by Oxley depot thirty-five years later. The shed was situated a little north of Cannock Road Junction, a mile north of Low Level station and adjacent to Dunstall Park station; it was visible to the left of the LNWR line from High Level station to Stafford.

Pressure on space at Stafford Road shed forced the GWR to build a new shed at Oxley to deal with freight traffic emanating from Wolverhampton and the Black Country. The new shed was opened in 1907 and was built of brick. It was situated adjacent to Wolverhampton racecourse, about ½ mile away from Stafford Road. The shed had several unusual features, not least the fact that because it was 25 ft above the natural ground level the shed walls were built on arches. The shed's turntables, of which there were two, were placed one behind the other because of the restrictions of the site. The narrow dimensions of the roundhouses, 181 ft 6 in by 450 ft, gives some idea of how tight the area was in which the shed was situated. The only alteration made to the shed was the provision of an extra coal tip, which replaced the last window of the coaling stage.

The two sheds retained their importance until the demise of steam, when it became clear that Stafford Road was surplus to requirements. The shed closed in September 1963 and locomotives for local use were then supplied by Oxley. The shed, along with the loco works, was demolished shortly afterwards, the land being given over to industrial use. Oxley shed only survived for another three and a half years, closing in March 1967.

The LNWR shed was situated at Bushbury, just over 1½ miles from High Level station. The shed replaced a small structure that had been situated close to the station but which had gradually fallen into disrepair since 1852. There was an urgent need for new shed accommodation and this new depot was built in July 1859 at a cost of £2,150 and had an allocation of twelve locos. Another shed was built in 1882 and accommodated twenty-four engines. This shed was provided with a 42-ft turntable and one approach road, which often led to blockages. It remained open until 12 April 1965 and was demolished soon after, the site being used as a gypsy caravan site from 1974.

Although the former LNWR route was the only surviving main line route through Wolverhampton, the GWR still had the final word as far as loco sheds were concerned, their Oxley shed outliving the former LNWR shed at Bushbury by some two years.

Stafford Road Shed Allocations

Codes:	GWR	SRD
	BR	84A

June 1947

'Wolverhampton'	0–6–0PT	1863, 2061, 2067, 2095, 2109, 2110, 2156, 2791
Collett	0–6–0PT	3615, 3756, 3760, 3778, 5739, 6418, 6422, 8705, 8726, 8734, 9621
Collett Goods	0–6–0	2231, 2232
Churchward	2–6–2T	3160, 4101, 4103, 4105, 4108, 4110, 4115, 5111, 5143, 5151
Churchward	2–6–0	6321, 6391, 7315
Collet	2–6–0	5909, 5919, 5927, 5942, 5944, 5995
Robinson ROD	2–8–0	3008, 3020, 3043
'County' class	4–6–0	1016 'County of Hants', 1017 'County of Hereford' 1024 'County of Pembroke' 1025 'County of Radnor' 1029 'County of Worcester'
'Star' class	4–6–0	4018 'Knight of the Grand Cross' 4025 'Italian Monarch' 4031 'Queen Mary' 4053 'Princess Alexandra' 4060 'Princess Eugenie'
'Castle' class	4–6–0	4000 'North Star' 5015 'Kingswear Castle' 5018 'St Mawes Castle' 5031 'Totnes Castle' 5033 'Broughton Castle' 5053 'Earl Cairns' 5070 'Sir Daniel Gooch' 5075 'Wellington' 5088 'Llanthony Abbey' 7007 'Great Western'
'King' class	4–6–0	6005 'King George II' 6006 'King George I'

		6008 'King James II'
		6011 'King James I'
'Hall' class	4–6–0	4960 'Pyle Hall'
		6901 'Arley Hall'
		6908 'Downham Hall'
		6924 'Grantley Hall'
		6964 'Thornbridge Hall'
'Grange' class	4–6–0	6844 'Penhydd Grange'
		6848 'Toddington Grange'
		6856 'Stowe Grange'

Total: 75

31 December 1947, the last day of GWR ownership

'Wolverhampton'	0–6–0PT	1863, 2061, 2067, 2095, 2109, 2110, 2156, 2791
Collett	0–6–0PT	3756, 3760, 3778, 5739, 6418, 6422, 8705, 8726, 8734, 9621
Collett Goods	0–6–0	2232
Churchward	2–6–2T	3102, 3160, 4103, 4105, 4108, 4110, 4115, 5103, 5111, 5143, 5151
Churchward	2–6–0	6321, 6391, 7315
Robinson ROD	2–8–0	3008, 3020, 3043
'County' class	4–6–0	1016 'County of Hants'
		1017 'County of Hereford'
		1024 'County of Pembroke'
		1025 'County of Radnor'
		1029 'County of Worcester'
'Star' class	4–6–0	4018 'Knight of the Grand Cross'
		4025 'Italian Monarch'
		4031 'Queen Mary'
		4053 'Princess Alexandra'
		4060 'Princess Eugenie'
'Castle' class	4–6–0	4000 'North Star'
		5015 'Kingswear Castle'
		5018 'St Mawes Castle'
		5031 'Totnes Castle'
		5053 'Earl Cairns'
		5070 'Sir Daniel Gooch'
		5075 'Wellington'
		5088 'Llanthony Abbey'
		7007 'Great Western'
'King' class	4–6–0	6005 'King George II'
		6006 'King George I'
		6008 'King James II'
		6011 'King James I'
'Hall' class	4–6–0	4950 'Patshull Hall'
		4960 'Pyle Hall'
		5909 'Newton Hall'
		5919 'Worsley Hall'
		5927 'Guild Hall'
		5942 'Doldowlod Hall'
		5944 'Ickenham Hall'
		5995 'Wick Hall'
		6901 'Arley Hall'
		6908 'Downham Hall'
		6924 'Grantley Hall'

		6964 'Thornbridge Hall'
'Grange' class	4–6–0	6812 'Chesford Grange'
		6844 'Penhydd Grange'
		6848 'Toddington Grange'

Total: 74

February 1954

Collett	0–6–0PT	3615, 3664, 3756, 3778, 3792, 3793, 5739, 5780, 8705, 8726, 8734, 8798, 9621
Collett	0–6–2T	5634, 6418, 6422
Hawksworth	0–6–0PT	8411, 8462, 9428, 9435
Churchward	2–6–2T	3102, 3104, 4103, 4108, 5106, 5112, 5151, 5187, 5188
Churchward	2–6–0	7309
'County' class	4–6–0	1004 'County of Somerset'
		1018 'County of Leicester'
		1019 'County of Merioneth'
'Star' class	4–6–0	4053 'Princess Alexandra'
		4061 'Glastonbury Abbey'
'Castle' class	4–6–0	4000 'North Star'
		4079 'Pendennis Castle'
		4083 'Abbotsbury Castle'
		4090 'Dorchester Castle'
		4092 'Dunraven Castle'
		5008 'Raglan Castle'
		5010 'Restormel Castle'
		5015 'Kingswear Castle'
		5022 'Wigmore Castle'
		5027 'Farleigh Castle'
		5031 'Totnes Castle'
		5032 'Usk Castle'
		5045 'Earl of Dudley'
		5053 'Earl Cairns'
		5070 'Sir Daniel Gooch'
		5088 'Llanthony Abbey'
		7026 'Tenby Castle'
'King' class	4–6–0	6004 'King George III'
		6005 'King George II'
		6006 'King George I'
		6011 'King James I'
		6016 'King Edward V'
		6020 'King Henry IV'
'Hall' class	4–6–0	4997 'Elton Hall'
		6949 'Haberfield Hall'
		6964 'Thornbridge Hall'

Total: 61

Oxley Shed Allocations

Codes:	GWR	OXY
	BR	84B
		2B (from 9/63)

June 1947

'Wolverhampton'	0–6–0PT	1762
Collett	0–6–0PT	3744, 3745, 3792, 3793, 5748, 5780, 7759, 7796,

		7797, 8798, 9714, 9715, 3730, 9739, 9742, 9747, 9752, 9768, 9769
Hawksworth	0–6–0PT	9408
Collett	0–6–2T	5657, 5670, 5684, 6600, 6609, 6610, 6640, 6645
Churchward	2–6–2T	3102, 3104
Collett	2–8–2T	7207, 7222, 7226, 7227, 7236, 7238, 7240, 7243, 7248
'Aberdare' double-framed	2–6–0	2623, 2665
Churchward	2–6–0	5300, 5313, 5331, 5333, 5379, 5386, 5390, 6332, 6335, 6342, 6361, 6362, 7307, 7311, 7317, 9312, 9314
Churchward	2–8–0	2825, 2830, 4708
Robinson ROD	2–8–0	3016, 3024, 3031, 3033, 3039
'Hall' class	4–6–0	4904 'Binnegar Hall'
		4916 'Crumlin Hall'
		4923 'Evenley Hall'
		4944 'Middleton Hall'
		4950 'Patshull Hall'
		4955 'Plaspower Hall'
		4964 'Rodwell Hall'
		4987 'Brockley Hall'
		4996 'Eden Hall'
		5916 'Trinity Hall'
		5918 'Walton Hall'
		5920 'Wycliffe Hall'
		5921 'Bingley Hall'
		5945 'Leckhampton Hall'
		5947 'Saint Benet's Hall'
		5957 'Hutton Hall'
		5989 'Cransley Hall'
		6915 'Mursley Hall'
		6932 'Burwarton Hall'
		6939 'Calveley Hall'
		6942 'Eshton Hall'
		6956 'Mottram Hall'
		6967 'Willesley Hall'
		6970 'Whaddon Hall'
'Grange' class	4–6–0	6862 'Derwent Grange'
		6879 'Overton Grange'
'Manor' class	4–6–0	7813 'Freshford Manor'
WD	2–8–0	77012, 77014, 77026, 77028, 77040, 77049, 77064, 77077, 77079, 77097, 77202, 77234, 77257, 77297, 77408, 78604, 78695, 78714, 79219, 79224, 79225
LMS 8F	2–8–0	8478

Total: 116

31 December 1947, the last day of GWR ownership

'Wolverhampton'	0–6–0PT	1762, 2713
Collett	0–6–0PT	3744, 3745, 3792, 3793, 5740, 5780, 7759, 7796, 7797, 8798, 9714, 9715, 9730, 9739, 9742, 9747, 9752, 9768, 9769
Hawksworth	0–6–0PT	9408
Collett	0–6–2T	5606, 5657, 5670, 5684, 6600, 6609, 6610, 6638, 6640, 6645
Churchward	2–6–2T	3104
Collett	2–8–2T	7207, 7222, 7226, 7227, 7236, 7238, 7240, 7243, 7248

'Aberdare' double-framed	2–6–0	2623, 2665
Churchward	2–6–0	5300, 5313, 5331, 5333, 5379, 5386, 5390, 6332, 6335, 6361, 6362, 7307, 7311, 7317, 7319, 9312, 9314
Churchward	2–8–0	2825, 2830, 4708
Robinson ROD	2–8–0	3016, 3024, 3031, 3033, 3039
'Hall' class	4–6–0	4904 'Binnegar Hall'
		4916 'Crumlin Hall'
		4923 'Evenley Hall'
		4944 'Middleton Hall'
		4955 'Plaspower Hall'
		4964 'Rodwell Hall'
		4987 'Brockley Hall'
		4991 'Cobham Hall'
		4996 'Eden Hall'
		5916 'Trinity Hall'
		5918 'Walton Hall'
		5920 'Wycliffe Hall'
		5921 'Bingley Hall'
		5945 'Leckhampton Hall'
		5947 'Saint Benet's Hall'
		5957 'Hutton Hall'
		5979 'Cruckton Hall'
		5989 'Cransley Hall'
		6915 'Mursley Hall'
		6932 'Burwarton Hall'
		6939 'Calveley Hall'
		6942 'Eshton Hall'
		6956 'Mottram Hall'
		6967 'Willesley Hall'
		6970 'Whaddon Hall'
		6975 'Capesthorne Hall'
'Grange' class	4–6–0	6856 'Stowe Grange'
		6862 'Derwent Grange'
		6879 'Overton Grange'
'Manor' class	4–6–0	7813 'Freshford Manor'
WD	2–8–0	77028, 77040, 77049, 77064, 77079, 77151, 77165, 77202, 77234, 78695, 79219, 79225

Total: 111

February 1954

Collett	0–6–0PT	3694, 3744, 3745, 7759, 7796, 9714, 9715, 9730, 9739, 9752, 9768
Hawksworth	0–6–0PT	8428, 9408
Collett	0–6–2T	5684, 6600, 6610, 6640, 6645
Churchward	2–6–0	5331, 5336, 5341, 5375, 5378, 5381, 5390, 5391, 6324, 6335, 6355, 9307, 9312, 9314, 9317, 9318
Churchward	2–8–0	2830, 2833, 2841, 2854, 2882, 3802, 3813, 3825, 3860, 3863, 3865
Robinson ROD	2–8–0	3016, 3028, 3029, 3031
'Hall' class	4–6–0	4918 'Dartington Hall'
		4919 'Donnington Hall'
		4924 'Eydon Hall'
		4926 'Fairleigh Hall'
		4955 'Plaspower Hall'

		4959 'Purley Hall'
		5944 'Ickenham Hall'
		5945 'Leckhampton Hall'
		5966 'Ashford Hall'
		5972 'Olton Hall'
		5991 'Gresham Hall'
		5995 'Wick Hall'
		6924 'Grantley Hall'
		6926 'Holkham Hall'
		6942 'Eshton Hall'
		6975 'Capesthorne Hall'
		7915 'Mere Hall'
'Grange' class	4–6–0	6854 'Roundhill Grange'
		6856 'Stowe Grange'
		6861 'Crynant Grange'
		6862 'Derwent Grange'
		6879 'Overton Grange'

Total: 71

+ diesel shunters 13034, 13035, 13036, 13037, 13038, 13039

Total: 6

Bushbury Shed Allocations

Codes:	LMS and BR	3B
	1960 –	21C
	1963 –	2K

November 1945

Fowler	2–6–2T	49, 53, 54, 66
Stanier	2–6–4T	2489
LMS 4F	0–6–0	4027, 4439, 4492
LMS class 5P5F	4–6–0	5287, 5405, 5437
LMS class 5XP		
'Patriot' class	4–6–0	5502 'Royal Naval Division'
		5511 'Isle of Man'
		5512 'Bunsen'
		5513
		5515 'Caernarvon'
		5522 'Prestatyn'
		5531 'Sir Frederick Harrison'
		5533 'Lord Rathmore'
LNWR 1P	2–4–2T	6652
LNWR 1P	2–6–2T	6933, 6935
LMS class 3F	0–6–0T	7397, 7398, 7399, 7413, 7473
LNWR	0–8–0	9011, 9110, 9204, 9206, 9233, 9236, 9295, 9356
LNWR 17"	0–6–0	28209, 28216, 28230, 28234
LNWR 18"	0–6–0	28403, 28430

Total: 41

November 1950

Fowler	2–6–2T	40047, 40049, 40053, 40066
Ivatt	2–6–2T	41225
LMS 4F	0–6–0	44027, 44439, 44492

LMS class 5	4–6–0	45015, 45287, 45405, 45434, 45437
LMS class 6P 'Jubilee' class	4–6–0	45703 'Thunderer' 45741 'Leinster'
LMS class 7P 'Royal Scot' class	4–6–0	46110 'Grenadier Guardsman' 46140 'The King's Royal Rifle Corps' 46148 'The Manchester Regiment' 46151 'The Royal Horse Guardsman' 46163 'Civil Service Rifleman' 46165 'The Ranger (12th London Regt.)
LMS class 3F	0–6–0T	47397, 47398, 47399, 47473
Ex-LNWR	0–8–0	48902, 48940, 49037, 49044, 49162, 49167, 49196, 49204, 49240, 49346
Ex-MR 2F	0–6–0	58119, 58152, 58285, 58286, 58287

Total: 40

+ diesel shunters		12039, 12040, 12041, 12042, 12043, 12044, 12059, 12060, 12061, 12062, 12074, 12075, 12076, 12077

Total: 14

January 1954

Fowler	2–6–2T	40064
Stanier 2–6–2T	40084, 40122, 40125, 40207	
Ivatt	2–6–2T	41225
LMS 4F	0–6–0	44027, 44439, 44492
LMS class 5	4–6–0	44829, 45015, 45287, 45405
LMS class 6P 'Jubilee' class	4–6–0	45647 'Sturdee' 45688 'Polyphemus' 45703 'Thunderer' 45733 'Novelty' 45734 'Meteor' 45737 'Atlas' 45738 'Samson' 45741 'Leinster' 45742 'Connaught'
LMS class 3F	0–6–0T	47363, 47397, 47398, 47473
Ex-LNWR	0–8–0	48940, 49037, 49044, 49125, 49167, 49240, 49247
Ex-MR 2F	0–6–0	58119, 58152, 58183

Total: 36

+ diesel shunters		12039, 12040, 12041, 12042, 12043, 12044, 12059, 12060, 12061, 12062, 12074, 12075, 12076, 12077

Total: 14

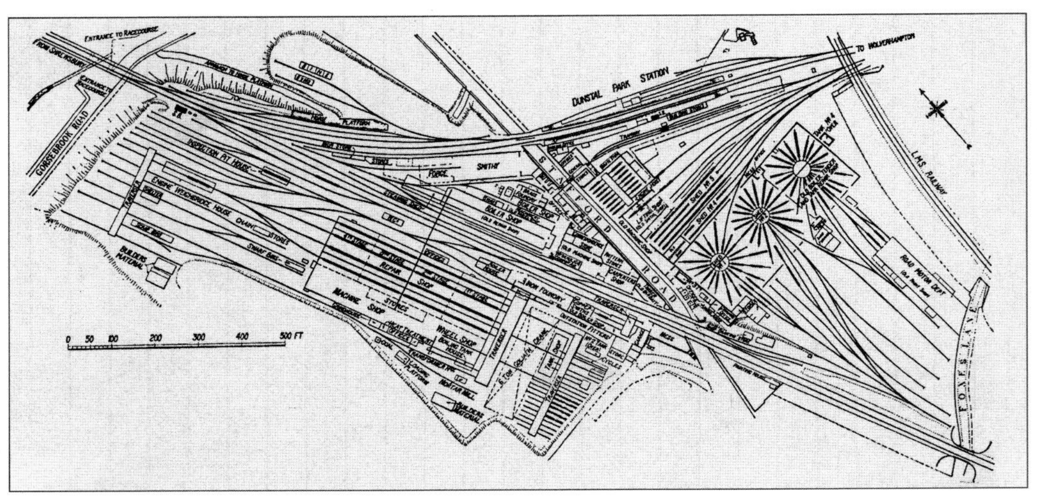

A plan of Stafford Road loco shed after it was modernised in the early 1930s. The work was funded by the 1929 Loans and Guarantee Act, which was instituted in an effort to provide work for the unemployed as the effects of the Great Depression began to be felt. A new large locomotive workshop was built and completed in 1932. Also the 35 ft by 120 ft two-road straight shed immediately behind the first roundhouse and the 67 ft by 250 ft four-road straight shed next to it were rebuilt as steel-framed, corrugated covered structures. At about the same time the final coaling stage, beyond the LMS High Level line, was constructed. As water tanks were already sited within the main shed complex, the two-road ramp approach was roofed with a single pitch slate roof. A turntable was also installed beyond the end of the ramp. The roundhouse nearest to the LMS main line was used as a tank repair shop for a few years and, later on, fell into a state of disrepair, as did the roundhouse next to it. A shed for GWR lorries and buses was also situated opposite the tank repair shop.

A panoramic view of Stafford Road shed, with Dunstall Park station on the right and Stafford Road loco works behind, 10 September 1957. On the left of the view are Collett 'Castle' class 4–6–0s with Collett 'Hall' or 'Grange' class 4–6–0s in the centre and various tank locos on the right. From its earliest days the shed assumed an important role, Wolverhampton being the point where locos were changed on trains running between Paddington and Birkenhead, not least because of the change of gauge at Wolverhampton. When the whole line was narrowed, Wolverhampton retained this role, Northern Division and Southern Division boundaries being located here. From 1900 to 1910 express engines of the Southern Division were usually 4–2–2 singles, which ran Paddington trains as far as Wolverhampton where Northern Division 2–4–0s took trains on to Shrewsbury and Birkenhead. Stafford Road, therefore, always housed top-link locomotives of both divisions for use on these trains. Over the years, the allocation included four-cylinder 'Star', 'Castle' and 'King' class 4–6–0s, as well as two-cylinder 'Saint', 'Hall', 'Grange' and 'County' class locos and the usual 0–6–0 pannier tanks and goods locos.

Stafford Road shed and staff with Churchward four-cylinder 'Star' class 4–6–0 No. 4067 *Tintern Abbey*. The loco was built in January 1923 and was almost certainly new when this picture was taken. It retained its inside steam pipes throughout its life, being withdrawn in September 1940 after seventeen years of service. It was rebuilt as 'Castle' class loco No. 5087 and retained its original name, finally going for scrap in August 1963. In GWR days, the shed codes were painted on the frame adjacent to the buffer beam of locos and in BR days on an oval cast plate attached to the bottom of the smokebox door. Both Stafford Road and Oxley locos carried the code WPN until 1920 when Stafford Road was given the code SRD and Oxley OXY. Following nationalisation, Western Region sheds were given the first number coding of 8, followed by another number to denote its division, followed by a letter to show the parent shed. Thus Stafford Road became 84A and Oxley 84B. These codes remained in use until 1963 when WR sheds in the West Midlands were transferred to the London-Midland Region. Oxley, then the only ex-GWR shed in Wolverhampton, became 2B from September 1963. The GWR had only used numerical shed codings for administrative purposes, the locos never carrying these numbers. Under this system, Stafford Road was numbered 194 and Oxley 114.

Outside the old Stafford Road shed is GWR Churchward 2–6–2 Prairie tank No. 3120, mid-1920s. A loco boiler and a set of locomotive driving wheels can be seen on the left in the background.

Dean double-framed 0–6–0 goods loco No. 1195, a relic from the nineteenth century is taking on water at the Stafford Road shed, July 1931. Judging by the brickwork in this view, the shed looks to be newly built.

Churchward 'Star' class 4–6–0 No. 4043 *Prince Henry* in the yard outside the newly constructed Stafford Road loco shed, *c.* 1935. Adjacent to the express loco appears to be a double-framed 'Bulldog' class 4–4–0 passenger engine and to the left of that, a 2–6–2 Prairie tank.

'Star' class 4–6–0 No. 4057 *Princess Elizabeth* in the Stafford Road shed yard, 1935. The loco was built in July 1914 and withdrawn as late as October 1957 – she was one of the last of her class to survive.

Churchward 2–6–0 Mogul No. 5317 rests outside Stafford Road shed, 1935. These locos were the mainstay of freight traffic in the area and throughout the GWR system until withdrawal of the class in the early 1960s. Behind the Mogul is an unidentified GWR 2–8–2 tank engine used for heavy freight work and common in the South Wales coalfields.

Ex-GWR 2–6–2 Prairie tank No. 3160 heads a coal train out of Stafford Road shed yard, 4 September 1949. The shed buildings are visible in the background.

'Hall' class 4–6–0 No. 4900 *Saint Martin* at the coaling stage, Stafford Road shed, late 1950s. This loco was rebuilt from Churchward's 'Saint' class, introduced in 1902 and fitted with 6-ft wheels instead of the 'Saint's' 6 ft 8½ in wheels. She became the prototype for the famous Collett 'Hall' class of 4–6–0 and survived in this condition until being scrapped in 1959.

Ex-GWR 'Castle' class 4–6–0 No. 4094 *Dynevor Castle* rests in Stafford Road shed yard, late 1950s. Following nationalisation, both Stafford Road and Oxley sheds retained their importance until modernisation drastically reduced the number of steam locomotives operating in the Wolverhampton area. The Western Region was, after all, the first of the regions to fully dieselise its operations, which was achieved by 1966. The WR 'Western' diesel-hydraulic locos could operate from Paddington right through to Birkenhead without the need to change at Wolverhampton. Consequently, Stafford Road lost its important function although some 'King' class locos were steamed each day to cover for possible diesel failures. It soon became clear, however, that Stafford Road shed was surplus to requirements and it closed in September 1963; if any locos were required after this date they were supplied by Oxley shed. Virtually all of the shed's allocation of 'King' and 'Castle' locos were sent to the scrapyard.

Standing outside the coaling stage at Stafford Road shed is 'Castle' class 5026 *Criccieth Castle*, 1960. This engine was one of the members of the class fitted with a double chimney in the early 1950s. While the double chimney did much to better the performance of the locos, it did little to improve their appearance.

'Castle' class 4–6–0 No. 5056 *Earl of Powis* and Collett 0–6–0 pannier tank No. 4683 outside a dilapidated Stafford Road shed, early 1960s. The two roads running between No. 1 shed of the former broad gauge shed at Stafford Road were roofed over in the mid-1860s to provide additional accommodation. This became known as 'The Arcade' or No. 4 shed.

Hawksworth 'Hall' class 4–6–0 No. 6944 *Fledborough Hall* with straight-sided Hawksworth tender at Stafford Road shed yard, early 1960s. In the background is an unidentified 'Castle' 4–6–0.

Doyen of the famous 'King' class 4–6–0, No. 6000 *King George V* resting in Stafford Road shed yard, late 1950s. It is complete with the bell it was awarded when it travelled to the USA in 1926. By this time the engine had been fitted with a double chimney, as had the rest of the thirty members of the class.

Rear of No. 6000 *King George V* at Stafford Road. The two medals that were also awarded to the train on the trip to the USA are seen on the side of the cab.

Another 'King' class loco, No. 6009 *King Charles II*, at Stafford Road shed yard, late 1950s.

'Castle' class 4–6–0 No. 7024 *Powis Castle* at Stafford Road, late 1950s. The GWR Collett 'Castle' class locos had been allocated to Stafford Road shed since 1932 when the Wolverhampton–Chester route had been given a 'red' classification, which meant that any class of loco, except the 'Kings', could be used over the route.

No. 7027 *Thornbury Castle*, another of the famous 'Castle' class that were the mainstay of the express fleet at Stafford Road. This locomotive was one of the class built by the Western Region in the early 1950s – not bad for a design introduced in 1923.

Ex-LMS 4P Compound 4–4–0 No. 41123 on a special to the Talyllyn Railway in Mid Wales passes the coal stage at Stafford Road loco shed, 1956. An 0–6–0 pannier tank is in the background. At this time this now London-Midland Region loco was an unusual sight at Wolverhampton, but it was, perhaps, a portent of things to come.

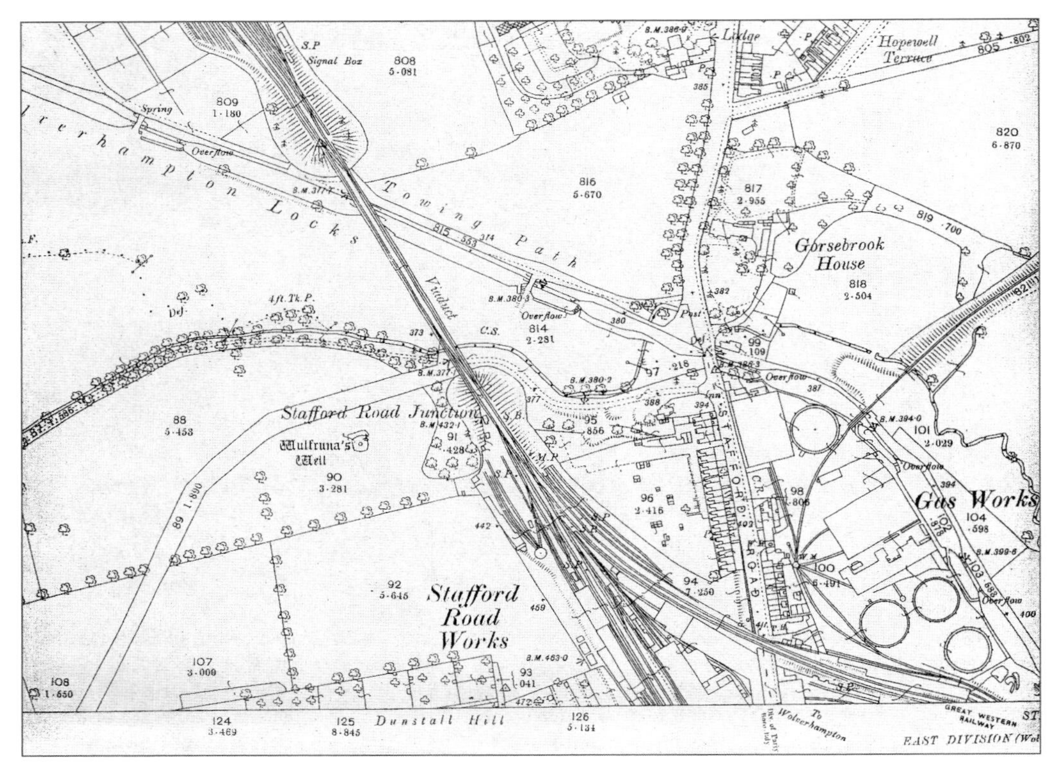

A map showing the works and shed at Stafford Road and the ex-Shrewsbury & Birmingham Railway as far as the major freight sidings at Oxley, 1880s.

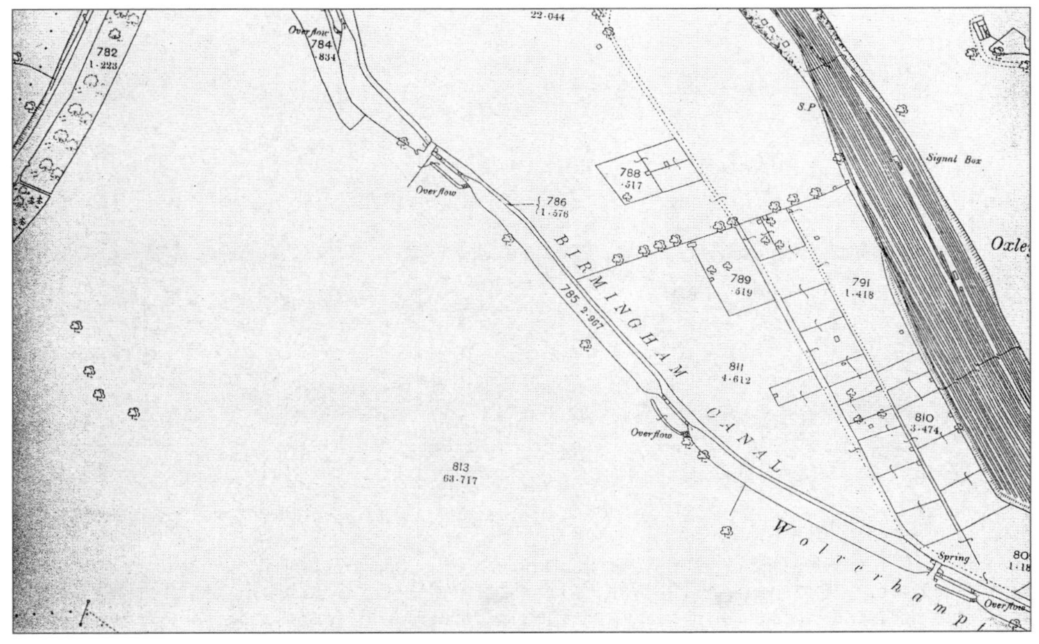

A map showing the sidings at Oxley and the reason why a new loco shed would eventually be placed there – a large goods yard was developed here and Stafford Road loco shed found it difficult to provide engines for freight traffic emanating from the Oxley yard, 1880s.

The interior of Oxley shed, 1935. On the right is ex-ROD 2–8–0 No. 3039, a Robinson design of the Great Central Railway and, on the left, GWR Churchward 2–6–0 Mogul No. 8341. Like Stafford Road, Oxley was fitted with a 65-ft undergirder turntable. The shed also had a lifting shop fitted with a 35-ton hoist to enable its allocation of locomotives to be maintained. Offices were incorporated in part of a two-storey general stores building. When the shed was originally built, provision was made for a further two turntables to be added on the main line side of the depot, which partly explains why, in comparison with other GWR sheds, the coaling stage was set back. Locomotive allocations at Oxley reflected the nature of traffic dealt with at the shed: mixed traffic two-cylinder 4–6–0s, 2–6–0 and 2–8–0 freight tender engines, 2–6–2 and 2–8–2 tank engines, as well as a few 0–6–0 pannier tanks. In the years immediately after the Second World War ex-WD 2–8–0 tender engines were also shedded there along with the occasional LMS 8F 2–8–0.

Churchward 2–6–0 loco No. 5300 at Oxley shed yard, 1949. This photograph was taken during the early BR Western Region days and the loco has been fitted with a cast smokebox number plate but has yet to receive its British Railways 'lion and wheel' badge; the old GWR markings have been removed. During the Second World War, Oxley shed was provided with ash shelters, which were built over the coaling roads solely to conceal the glow of discarded firebox coal from observation by enemy aircraft during the nightly 'blackout'. These ash shelters were built of a light steel frame with the lower half of the walls being constructed of brick, the remainder being sheeted, and a corrugated roof. The overall dimensions of these ash shelters was 35 ft by 100 ft.

Ex-GWR Collett 0–6–2 tank loco outside Oxley shed, 4 September 1949. These locos were a more common sight on lines in the South Wales coalfields. Some locomotives were transferred between Oxley and Stafford Road from time to time. For example, 'Grange' class 4–6–0 No. 6856 *Stowe Grange* was allocated to Stafford Road in June 1947 but had been assigned to Oxley by the following December. 'Hall' class 4–6–0 No. 4950 *Patshull Hall* made the opposite transfer in the same period, being allocated to Oxley in June 1947 and to Stafford Road in December 1947.

Dean Goods 0–6–0 No. 2408 of nineteenth-century vintage looking somewhat the worse for wear inside Oxley shed, 4 September 1949.

Standing alongside the coaling stage at Oxley shed is Collett 'Grange' class 4–6–0 No. 6874 *Haughton Grange*, 1958.

'Grange' class loco No. 6839 *Hewell Grange* is in the shed yard at Oxley, with the giant goods yard, the reason for the shed's existence, in the background. The closure of Oxley shed in March 1967 brought to an end the premier status enjoyed by the GWR in Wolverhampton. This situation would have delighted the old enemy of the Paddington company, Captain Mark Huish, the former General Manager of the LNWR who had tried so hard to prevent the Great Western Railway ever reaching the town.

The coaling plant at Bushbury shed, July 1947. This was built as part of a modernisation project in 1936, which also included a new ash-handling plant and 70-ft turntable. A water softener was also meant to be installed at the shed in 1939 but the Second World War intervened and it was not put in place until 1946. Roof renewal was also due to have been undertaken before the war but this had to be left until the shed came under BR control. In LMS days, the shed was coded 3B until recoding in 1960, when it became 21C (a subshed of Saltley, Birmingham), becoming 2K from September 1963.

Ex-LMS 'Jinty' 0–6–0 tank loco No. 47473 is on coaling duties, while the coaling plant is under repair, near the turntable at Bushbury shed, 1 May 1949. In 1882, a new loco shed was built at Bushbury which could accommodate twenty-four engines. This new shed was of the standard LNWR type, built of brick with a north-light pattern roof, and had eight straight roads. Unfortunately the layout was poor, possibly based on that of the original shed yard, and to enter the yard, coal and stable in the shed involved eight separate movements: four forward and four in reverse. To add to the problems there, queues and blockages arose because the 42-ft turntable had only one approach road. In 1876 there were forty-two engines stabled in Bushbury but Monument Lane shed in Birmingham supplied all locos used on Euston services even though some ran from Wolverhampton. In 1905, however, this duty passed to Bushbury and to cope with larger engines a new 50-ft turntable was supplied at the shed. While Monument Lane took on the role of supplying locos for Euston services during the Second World War, the duty reverted to Bushbury during peacetime.

Ex-Midland Railway 0–6–0 No. 58183, with old MR-type tender, at Bushbury shed, 15 January 1952. These former Midland engines replaced ex-LNWR 0–6–0 coal engines after nationalisation.

Bushbury shed yard with ex-LMS Stanier 'Jubilee' class 4–6–0 No. 45733 *Novelty* to the right, 13 June 1957.

'Princess-Coronation' Pacific No. 46248 *City of Leeds* at Bushbury, 1962. This was an unusual sight at Bushbury as these Pacifics usually operated Glasgow–Euston expresses, which never ran through Wolverhampton. Over the years allocations at Bushbury increased until they reached a peak of nearly sixty just after the 'Grouping'. From that point numbers began to decline until, by 1954, only some thirty-eight engines were allocated at Bushbury, including two of the new diesel shunters. Among the locos allocated to Bushbury at this time were 2–6–2 tanks of Stanier, Fowler and Ivatt types, with four 'Jinty' tanks. Ex-Midland Railway engines at the shed included three Johnson 0–6–0s and three LMS-built 4F 0–6–0s of Midland parentage. Ex-LNWR types still based at the shed at this time were seven 0–8–0 heavy freight engines, necessary to deal with the coal and steel traffic that formed an essential part of goods traffic in Wolverhampton and the Black Country. Four 'Black 5' 4–6–0s were allocated to deal with mixed traffic turns. Seven 'Jubilee' class 4–6–0s were shedded at Bushbury for express passenger work, replacing 'Patriot' class 4–6–0s, which had been provided for Wolverhampton–Euston trains in LMS days. These 'Patriots' were always maintained in first-class condition by the Bushbury staff.

Ex-LNWR 'Super D' 0–8–0 engine No. 49452 outside Bushbury shed on a foggy day, 1962. These engines survived virtually until closure of the shed in 1965 and were the mainstay of heavy freight traffic in the Wolverhampton area after the end of the First World War.

CHAPTER SIX

STAFFORD ROAD LOCO WORKS

Construction of GWR locomotives has long been seen as the province of the Swindon works but the company also had another works at Wolverhampton. This works concentrated on building engines for narrow-gauge systems in the Northern Division, which had been acquired, or absorbed, by the GWR. The works were at Stafford Road and its products bore little relation to those broad-gauge and, later, narrow-gauge engines turned out at Swindon. Even the famous Brunswick Green livery, long associated with the GWR, was slightly different from that used at Swindon, the colour applied at Stafford Road having a slightly bluer hue when seen in sunlight. One notable feature of Wolverhampton locos, by which every GWR locomotive came to be recognised, was the brass safety valve bonnet, which was designed at Stafford Road. The works provided employment for thousands of local men over the years, even after locomotive construction ceased there in April 1908 and it was retained as a major centre for heavy repairs.

Workshops were originally established at Stafford Road by the Shrewsbury & Birmingham Railway in 1849. Facilities were extremely limited because the S&B was worked by contract, although the company did own the locomotives that were used, and therefore only repair work could be undertaken. The works were decimated by construction of the Wolverhampton Junction Railway in 1852, when most of the buildings were demolished to make way for the new line.

The S&B, along with the Shrewsbury & Chester Railway, were amalgamated to form the GWR in 1854. Joseph Armstrong, who had been in charge of all locomotive matters on the S&C, decided to establish responsibility for locomotive construction for what was to become the GWR's Northern Division at Wolverhampton. Carriage and wagon work were to become the speciality of the old S&C works at Saltney, near Chester.

Despite the importance of Swindon, Stafford Road was virtually an autonomous works. Joseph Armstrong was given a free hand in locomotive design and construction for the Northern Division, and Daniel Gooch became fully preoccupied with broad gauge matters. When Gooch retired from his position as Locomotive Superintendent at Swindon, in 1863, Joseph Armstrong took his place and left his younger brother, the formidable George, in charge at Wolverhampton along with a capable young engineer, William Dean. Dean, himself, moved to Swindon shortly afterwards, becoming Locomotive and Carriage Superintendent following the sudden death of Joseph Armstrong in 1877. George Armstrong having been his superior,

William Dean decided that it would not be politic to exert too much authority over him, which, inadvertently, gave Stafford Road a further twenty years of independence.

Despite losing its role as a manufacturer from 1908, Stafford Road Works was still important as a centre for heavy repair and maintenance work. Initially it dealt with everything except top-link express locomotives until after the Second World War, when the works did take on this type of work. After nationalisation, Stafford Road retained its status as a major repair centre and it was only when the effects of the 1955 'Modernisation Plan' began to be felt that the future of the works was threatened. At first, however, the works was to take on the role of maintaining the new diesel and electric locomotives that were coming on stream. But BR actually needed fewer of these new engines to run its trains and these types required less maintenance than the old steam locos they were replacing, which meant that fewer workshops were necessary and Wolverhampton's future was far from secure. Indeed, the works was finally closed in June 1964, ending 115 years of locomotive construction and maintenance in the town and marking the decline of Wolverhampton as a major railway centre in Britain.

Some Locomotive Classes Built at Stafford Road Works

Class	Type	Total Built	Dates Built
850			
1901	0–6–0T	170	1874–95
2021	0–6–0T	140	1897–1905
517	0–4–2ST	54	1868–85
517	0–4–2T	102	1868–85
517	0–4–2T	10[1]	1868–85
1016	0–6–0ST	60[2]	1867–71
45xx	2–6–2T	20	1906–8
Backwell tanks[3]	2–4–0T	12	1864–6

1. Slightly larger than the rest of the class.
2. These locos were rebuilt with Belpaire boilers and pannier tanks from 1911 onwards.
3. All later rebuilt with saddle tanks.

The remainder of new locomotives built at Stafford Road Works were 0–6–0 saddle tanks, with 4 ft 7½ in, or 4 ft 1½ in, driving wheels. Like the 1016 class locos, all but two were later fitted with Belpaire boilers and pannier tanks. Only loco numbers 1925 and 2007 retained saddle tanks throughout their lives until withdrawal in 1951 and 1949 respectively.

The interior of the new erecting shop at Stafford Road works. This new shop was built in the 1930s, along with a machine shop and wheel shop, on the Dunstall Hill site and was 450-ft long and 196-ft wide. The area in which the works was situated was very cramped, lying as it did between the GWR and LMS main lines. The site at Dunstall Hill had originally been bought in 1900, but as Swindon had become the most important centre for locomotive construction, the plans for the new works at Dunstall Hill were postponed. The land remained unused until the 1930s when the shop was constructed.

Ex-GWR Churchward 2–8–0 tank engine No. 4212 inside the erecting shop at Stafford Road works. In the days when Stafford Road was still constructing its own engines, the most obvious sign of the independence of the works from Swindon was the design of its 0–6–0 saddle tank engines, most of which were later converted into the ubiquitous pannier tanks. Swindon continued to build these and other locos as double-framed engines, while, from 1871, Wolverhampton went over to building inside-framed locos almost exclusively. Most of the engines manufactured at Stafford Road were 0–4–2 and 0–6–0 tanks. The works was also involved in rebuilding engines from the old absorbed companies, some of which created as much work as building new engines. Between 1906 and 1908 Wolverhampton produced some small 2–6–2 Prairie tanks, one of which, No. 3519 (originally No. 2180 until rebuilt in 1912), was the last engine to be constructed at Stafford Road. Another engine of the same batch, No. 4507, was destined to be the last Wolverhampton-built locomotive to remain in service and was not withdrawn until October 1963. Up to April 1908, when all locomotive construction was concentrated on Swindon, the Stafford Road works produced 794 new engines and 102 rebuilds, which were so extensive that they could be considered as new. In addition, the works also built engines for six rail motors. In its heyday as loco builders, in excess of 1,500 men were employed at Stafford Road, making the works important within the local economy.

Ex-GWR 0–6–0 pannier tank, allocated to Stourbridge Junction, is undergoing an overhaul, 7 May 1950. Engines coming in for repair were put into sidings until they could be brought into the works where they were dealt with via a routing system, which classified them as light, intermediate or general repair. Locos were sent from various locations in the West Midlands on receipt of instructions from Swindon. The procedure at the works was that engines came into the shops at the south end where they were stripped down and, if a general repair was being undertaken, the boiler was removed from the frames. The boiler was then sent direct to the boiler shop, which was situated on the south side of the Victoria Goods line where a special track had been laid for the purpose. Once this was done the engine went into the repair shops and emerged some time later completely restored and ready for duties.

A GWR cast number plate from 0–6–0 pannier tank No. 1744 (one of the Wolverhampton-built saddle tanks converted to a pannier tank) of Wrexham Croes Newydd shed, 1935. The plate indicates that the engine was built at Wolverhampton in April 1892. The engine itself did not survive after nationalisation.

A group of loco men being educated about the workings of GWR engines at the Stafford Road works. In front of them are the remains (five pairs of wheels, inside cylinder valve gear and two-thirds of the frame) of ex-West Midland Railway 0–6–0 built by E.B. Wilson & Co. of Leeds in 1855. Its WMR (and OW&W) number was 34, and its GWR 252; the loco was withdrawn in August 1904.

GWR 'Castle' class 4–6–0 No. 5016 *Montgomery Castle*, complete with full Great Western crest and lettering on the tender, is on the traverser awaiting repair, 1930s. The works at Wolverhampton not only repaired everyday locos, but also the top-link 'Castle' and 'King' 4–6–0s.

War Department 0–6–0 No. 8182 is in the works yard at Stafford Road awaiting repair, 4 September 1949. During the Second World War, Stafford Road works undertook repairs on War Department locos, a practice that continued in the early years after the end of the war.

A pair of ex-War Department 0–6–0s, of uncertain age, in Stafford Road works yard awaiting repair.

An ex-LNWR coal engine as War Department No. 8108 0–6–0 at Stafford Road yard. What would Mark Huish have made of one of his company's engines awaiting repair in the works of his bitterest enemy? The engine was built at Crewe in 1874 and went to the Shropshire & Montgomery Railway in March 1930. The engine was transferred to the War Department in 1941.

Ex-LNWR No. 8108 at Stafford Road works, 1 May 1949. The engine was moved to Stafford Road early in 1949 and transferred to Western Region stock in May 1950. From Wolverhampton, the loco was moved to Swindon where it was finally scrapped in October 1950.

Ex-LNWR coal engine War Department No. 8236 at Stafford Road, 4 September 1949.

Stafford Road works yard with ex-GWR coaches in use as departmental vehicles, 1957. Departmental vehicles were used by the railway to carry staff to works as required; they were old passenger coaches.

A general view of the buildings and rail layout at Stafford Road works, 1950s. The boiler shop is on the left and the erecting shop on the right.

The last locomotive to be repaired at Stafford Road works before closure in June 1964. The engine was ex-GWR Churchward 2–8–0 No. 2859 allocated to Pontypool Road, South Wales for operating heavy coal trains from the coalfields. The engine was outshopped in February 1964, as the sign indicates, four months before the works were finally closed, which ended 115 years of locomotive construction and maintenance in Wolverhampton.

CHAPTER SEVEN

MODERNISATION

Following nationalisation, two railway reports were destined to have a profound effect on the railways at Wolverhampton. The first was the 1955 'Modernisation Plan', with its ideas to concentrate freight traffic into large marshalling yards and to bring about the demise of small goods yards, a number of which were scattered around the town. More importantly, as far as Wolverhampton was concerned, was the replacement of steam power with modern traction which eventually led to electrification of the West Coast Main Line and the Stafford–Wolverhampton (High Level)–Birmingham (New Street)–Euston route. Part of this plan also envisaged completely new stations at Stafford and Birmingham (New Street), along with complete rebuilding of Wolverhampton (High Level), to create a new image for what was to be a fully modern railway system.

The second report to make an impact was the infamous one submitted by Dr Beeching in 1963. It was a plan to rationalise Britain's railway system which would bring about the demise of the Western Region station at Low Level. This did not seem likely when most Wolverhampton–London trains were transferred from High Level to Low Level, from 2 November 1959, in order for electrification work to be undertaken and allow High Level station to be rebuilt. Even when Low Level station was transferred to London-Midland Region control in January 1963, staff had no reason to fear for the future of the station because it continued to be busy, handling about 130,000 trains a year in the early 1960s and dealing with some 7½ million passengers. However, within four years nearly all passenger services became concentrated on the new High Level station and Low Level was virtually redundant.

High Level station had certainly become rather dilapidated by the end of 1959, the structure having been in use for 108 years. The station was opened on 1 June 1852 and had a reputation for being a smoky, dingy, dirty, draughty and depressing 'hole'. A *Wolverhampton Express and Star* reporter who visited the station in November of that year described it thus: 'If High Level has a reputation, it is that of being the ugly sister of Low Level. The latter seems to fall naturally into its surroundings. High Level, alongside, seems to perch uneasily like a neurotic spinster on the edge of an unsavoury conversation.' Even BR admitted that a great deal of work needed to be carried out 'at this antiquated station' and that the exterior of High Level was the only good feature of the station.

Although the *Express and Star* reporter had commented that Low Level station was part of the landscape, its future had become uncertain. In April 1962, however, the situation looked different when new diesel-hydraulic locomotives were introduced on Paddington–Wolverhampton–Birkenhead expresses, which, it was hoped, would cut journey times between Wolverhampton and London to about 2¼ hours. However, from September of that year 'The Cornishman' express was transferred to the Birmingham (New Street)–Bristol route, avoiding Wolverhampton altogether. Local services from Low Level to Wellington were reduced and trains between Low Level and Stourbridge were withdrawn on 30 July 1962.

The demise of Low Level as an important express destination followed the completion of electrification at High Level and all express traffic was transferred to the newly electrified line. Loss of the Paddington–Birkenhead expresses was marked by special steam excursions operated by two preserved 'Castle' class locos, No. 4079 *Pendennis Castle* and No. 7029 *Clun Castle*, on 4 and 5 March 1967. This brought to an end over a century of express passenger trains at the old GWR station.

Wolverhampton (High Level) station with the goods yards and goods avoiding lines on the right, June 1960. Low Level station can be seen on the extreme right of the picture. High Level was the station described by the *Express and Star* reporter in such derogatory terms:

> The donkey's leg approach road from the town centre obscures the frontage and leads to what one traveller called 'a cross between a barracks and a wind tunnel'. This atmosphere is created by the slightly Wagnerian roof, a strident and overbearing structure in iron and glass, which has under its thumb a rather slender and wan collection of amenities – two waiting rooms, two newspaper stalls (one closed for most of the time) and only one buffet. There are few refinements. Certainly not, as at Low Level, a little cubicle where you can photograph yourself in three minutes (Four poses 2*s*).

Virtually all of the passengers interviewed by this intrepid reporter had nothing good to say about the station and all hoped that a new building would improve matters and electrification would make the whole area cleaner and brighter.

The frontage of the new High Level station shortly after it was opened and the electrification project completed, March 1967. Note the cars of the day parked outside, which include Ford Consul Classics, Mark One Cortinas and Corsairs. Almost as soon as the new station opened, it was the subject of complaints. The most vocal were concerned with the lack of cover over the platforms and the small number of waiting rooms, particularly on the island platform, and the shortage of refreshment facilities. Even BR was forced to admit that facilities at the new station were not as good as they should have been. The situation was made worse by the fact that passenger numbers at the new station had increased by 45 per cent, no doubt as a result of the withdrawal of Paddington expresses from Low Level station. In July 1967, BR announced that improvements were to be made at the station, which included increasing the number of waiting rooms and improving toilet facilities. Also, the awnings over the platform were extended by 130 ft. These were not the final improvements at the new station and in 1979 a new curved platform, numbered 10 and fully electrified, was opened. This terminal platform was used by trains operating from Shrewsbury and terminating at Wolverhampton.

New traction at Wolverhampton, 1974. Class 08 0–6–0 diesel shunter, No. 08 901 used on carriage movements, is seen at Wolverhampton station.

Electric loco class 86 Bo-Bo No. 86246 at rest in the sidings at Wolverhampton station. Following electrification, most express trains operating through Wolverhampton became electric hauled. Nowadays, while many expresses are electric hauled, some, especially those operating to the West Country, are run by diesel-electric 'Inter-City' 125 sets, which on the newly privatised railway are operated by Virgin Trains, as are WCML services. Local trains are made up of Sprinter DMUs operated by several private concerns. There is a class 37 hauled train, operated by North Western trains, running between Holyhead and Birmingham (New Street) via Wolverhampton.

A Wolverton-built coach of 1921, No. DM 395177, painted in blue on the bay at Wolverhampton station, 5 July 1975. Not many coaches of this era would have survived long enough to receive this electric-blue livery.

Back at Low Level, 9 May 1965. In the background, electrification of the High Level line to Birmingham (New Street) is in progress, although the old semaphore signal gantries are still in place to control the local train services that were still operating out of High Level station during the modernisation process. This view is just north of Low Level station and shows a cluster of buildings on the west side of the line.

Leaving Wolverhampton (Low Level) with an excursion to Ruabon and Portmadoc is ex-LNER Gresley A3 Pacific No. 4472 *Flying Scotsman*, then owned by Alan Pegler, 9 May 1965.

A Birmingham (Snow Hill) to Blackpool train leaves Low Level station behind a pair of English Electric Type 4 1Co-Co1 (later class 40) locos, Nos D213 and D221. The train will join the former LNWR line at Bushbury Junction. Owing to ongoing electrification work at High Level and Birmingham (New Street), trains for the north-west of England operated out of Snow Hill and ran over ex-GWR metals and gained the LMS route to Stafford and Crewe at Bushbury. Increasing demand at Snow Hill and Low Level was the grand swansong of the old GWR main line until all express services ceased in 1967.

A very depressing photograph of Wolverhampton (Low Level) station after all express traffic had ceased, Friday 1 March 1968. All Shrewsbury passenger services were transferred to High Level and nearby Dunstall Park station was closed, having become a haunt of tramps and vandals. After loss of the Shrewsbury services, the line between Stafford Road Junction and Low Level was lifted, leaving the ex-GWR station as a terminus operating DMU shuttles between Wolverhampton and Birmingham (Snow Hill); the front of one of these DMUs can be seen in the right-hand corner.

Low Level station and a Snow Hill shuttle. The shuttle operated until 4 March 1972 when Snow Hill was itself closed. At this time, Low Level station had become a parcels concentration depot, and opened as such on 6 April 1970 to serve an area from Lichfield to Kidderminster. It closed along with other depots when parcels-handling ceased in June 1981; the station was then abandoned. Despite having lost its rail traffic, Low Level station still exists and has been designated a Grade Two listed building and been repaired. There have been several suggestions for alternative uses for the building – as a museum or as a terminus for a light railway system from Birmingham now that Snow Hill has been reopened. However, nothing has resulted from any of these proposals. It seems a sad end for the once glorious GWR whose presence was such an important part of the social and economic life of Wolverhampton.